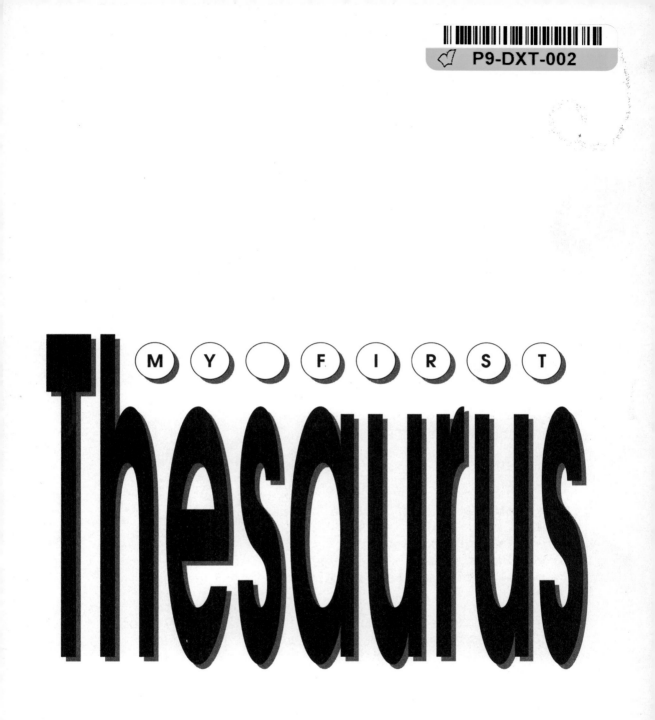

MY FIRST Thesaurus

Nelson Canada

Published in 1989 by
NELSON CANADA,
A Division of International Thomson Limited
1120 Birchmount Road
Scarborough, Ontario
M1K 5G4

ISBN 0 - 17 - 602998 - 2

First published in 1988 by
THE JACARANDA PRESS
65 Park Road, Milton, Qld 4064

Canadian Cataloguing in Publication Data

Main entry under title:

My first thesaurus

Includes index.
ISBN 0 - 17 - 602998 - 2

1. English language — Synonyms and antonyms — Juvenile literature.
2. English language — Dictionaries, Juvenile.

PE1591.M9 1989 j423'.1 C89 - 093659 - 5

General Editor: Leah Bloomfield

Contributing Editor: Barbara Bannon
Editor: Linda Bishop
Cover Design: John Robb
Cover Illustration: Jackie Snider
Internal Design and Illustration: Jennifer Marchant

Some words entered in this thesaurus may have been derived from trademarks. However, the presence or absence of this indication of derivation should not be regarded as affecting the legal status of any trademark.

Printed and bound in Canada
890 WC

Contents

Preface	iv
How to use the thesaurus	vi
'If at first you don't succeed...'	
A guide to the way some words start	vii
Guide to the thesaurus	viii
My First Thesaurus	1
Appendixes	175
Baby animals	176
Animals' homes	176
Male and female animals	176
Sounds animals make	177
Groups of animals	177
Land features	178
Water features	180
Quantity...	
words that tell you how much	181
Time...	
Words that tell you when	181
Index	183
Guide to the index	212

Preface

. . . for teachers and parents

My First Thesaurus is designed for children to use in the early years of elementary school, primarily seven- to ten-year-old children. It is written in an informal style and difficult words have been omitted so that children will be able to browse through it unaided if they wish. Guidance and encouragement, however, from teachers and parents will help ensure that young readers gain full benefit from their thesaurus.

Although *My First Thesaurus* looks very different from other thesauri, the information is arranged, for the most part, according to the same principles. That is, we have brought together a selection of words which are associated in meaning with one particular word — the **keyword**.

Those words which are so closely related that they can often be substituted for one another are grouped under a **heading**. Each heading indicates one particular sense in which the keyword may be understood. Below each heading is a sentence showing how the word is used to further clarify the meaning of the words in the group. Thus, along with the keyword **nice**, you will find the headings **pretty**, **delicious**, **kind**, **comfortable**, and so on, along with the words related to them.

Occasionally, as with the keywords **good** and **bad**, you will find a group of words that do not narrow down a particular sense of the keyword, but can be used in the most general way instead of the keyword. Thus, under the heading **more words that mean good** are *fabulous*, *great*, *splendid*, etc.

In other cases, as with the keyword **say**, under the heading **different ways you can say things**, you will find words such as *gasp*, *mumble*, *yell*, etc., which are specific and limited examples of usage of the keyword.

Some keywords, however, do not have lists of words arranged under headings. These pages list items that can be classified as members of the same group, but which cannot be substituted for one another. Thus the keyword **book** contains a list of different kinds of books, along with their definitions, as you would find in a dictionary.

My First Thesaurus differs from other thesauri at this level in offering such a wide range of meanings for each keyword. Thus, in the case of a keyword like **light** you will find a number of meanings: *illuminate*, *pale*, *light as a feather*, *catch fire*, and others. In choosing to include under the one keyword these various meanings, we recognize that young readers and writers do not yet understand differences in grammar and etymology, and to label words as different parts of speech or as homonyms would not be helpful to them.

We have not attempted to include every word in the child's vocabulary. The emphasis is on commonly used and over-used words, such as **good**, **bad**, **nice**, **do**, **get** and **say**. We have left out words for which the related words are too few or too difficult.

We hope that young readers and writers will enjoy using *My First Thesaurus* and that this will lead them to progress naturally to more adult-style thesauri.

How to use the thesaurus

I saw a really **good** *movie in the holidays. It was about a kid called Max who thought he wasn't very* **good** *at anything. One day a badly hurt pilot landed his plane near Max's house. He asked Max to help him fly back to the base. Max turned out to be a really* **good** *pilot. He made a* **good** *landing at the base and everyone cheered and said how* **good** *he was at flying and how* **good** *he had been to help. The pilot said Max could always count on him to be a* **good** *friend.*

Did you notice how many times the word **good** was repeated? Wouldn't the story sound more interesting if some other words were used instead? This is where *My First Thesaurus* can help.

A thesaurus is a book that has lists of words. In each list you will find words that have similar meanings. So, if you look up **good** on page 60–63 and write the story again using some of the words you find there, it might turn out something like this.

I saw a really **exciting** *movie in the holidays. It was about a kid called Max who thought he wasn't very* **clever** *at anything. One day a badly hurt pilot landed his plane near Max's house. He asked Max to help him fly back to the base. Max turned out to be a really* **great** *pilot. He made a* **perfect** *landing at the base and everyone cheered and said how* **skilful** *he was at flying and how* **kind** *he had been to help. The pilot said Max could always count on him to be a* **loyal** *friend.*

You can use your thesaurus like this when you are writing stories or letters. You will be able to find the lists for easy words like **bad, good,** and **nice** right away. They are in alphabetical order in the main part of the book. For other words you may need the index. If you don't know how to use an index, look at the last two pages of this book.

If there are any words in the lists that you don't know, look them up in your dictionary. A dictionary and a thesaurus go hand in hand.

'If at first you don't succeed'

. . . A guide to the way some words start

If you can't easily find the word you're looking up, it might be that the word begins with a letter or letters that you say in a different way to normal or which may be completely silent.

Here is a table to help you track down those tricky words.

Sound that the word begins with	The word could begin with this	Example
f	ph	photograph
g	gh	ghost
g	gu	guide
h	wh	whole
j	g	gem
k	ch	character
kw	qu	quite
n	gn	gnome
n	kn	knee
r	rh	rhyme
r	wr	write
s	c	cereal
s	sc	science
sh	s	sugar
sk	sch	school
w	wh	white
z	x	xylophone

Guide to the thesaurus

How many words can you think of that mean *big*? Look at the opposite page. Did you think of all of these?

Big is a word we often use, so we have made it a keyword in the thesaurus. The keyword is the main word on the page, so it is written in big blue letters.

The boxes contain other words with a similar meaning to the keyword. You can use these similar words instead of the keyword.

The keywords in the thesaurus are in alphabetical order. So if you want to find the keyword **big**, turn to the **b** section. There is **big** on page 7, in between **beautiful** on page 6 and **bold** on page 8.

It is easy to find words like **big**, **small**, **good**, and **bad** because they are keywords, but what would you do if the word you wanted wasn't a keyword?

Simple! Look it up in the index. Turn to the last two pages of this book to find out how to use the index.

heading — a word giving one of the meanings of the keyword

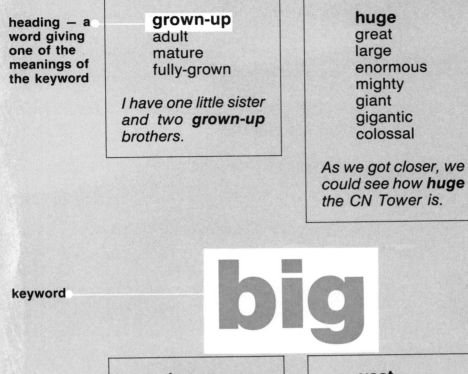

grown-up
adult
mature
fully-grown

*I have one little sister and two **grown-up** brothers.*

huge
great
large
enormous
mighty
giant
gigantic
colossal

*As we got closer, we could see how **huge** the CN Tower is.*

keyword

big

heavy
bulky
weighty

*This parcel is too **heavy** for me to carry.*

a sentence using the heading word

vast
huge
extensive
enormous
immense

*The Sahara is a **vast** desert.*

similar words — words you can use instead of the keyword or the heading word

START
1
2
3

regarding

*Our teacher wrote a letter to our parents **regarding** the swimming contest.*

about

nearly
almost
just about
practically

*I've **nearly** finished my work.*

roughly
more or less
approximately

*He's **roughly** the same size as you.*

?

cranky
grumpy
bad-tempered
irritable
snappy

*If I go to bed late I feel **cranky** the next day.*

furious
wild
worked up
hot and bothered

*Dad was really **furious** when someone crashed into our new car.*

angry

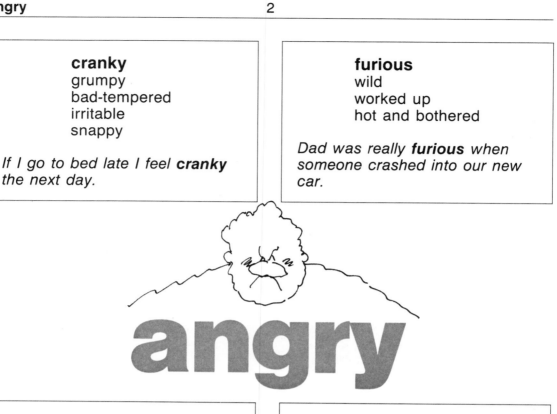

cross
annoyed
upset
mad

*Please don't be **cross**. It was an accident.*

sulky
hurt
put out
offended

*He's **sulky** because you didn't invite him to your party.*

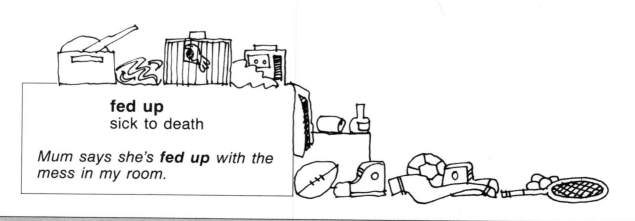

fed up
sick to death

*Mum says she's **fed up** with the mess in my room.*

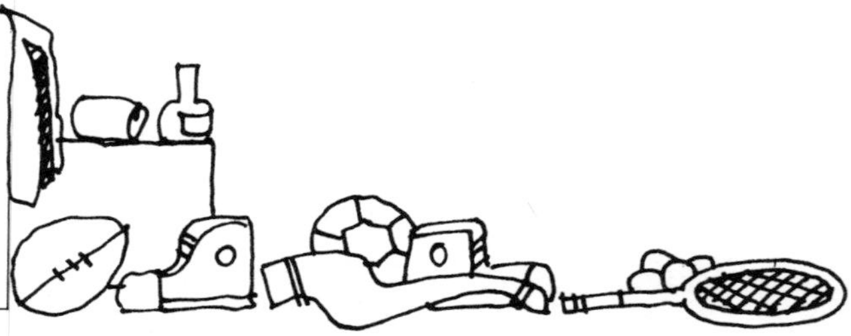

beg
plead

*I had to **beg** really hard to be allowed to go.*

order

*When the police **order** you to do something, you'd better obey.*

ask

question
quiz
cross-examine
interrogate

*The police had to **question** everyone who saw the accident.*

consult

*I don't know what this rash is. We'll have to **consult** the doctor.*

find out
enquire

*I'd like to **find out** how much that bike costs.*

request

*There are signs which **request** visitors not to feed the animals.*

dangerous
unsafe
risky
hazardous

*It's **dangerous** to cross the road without looking first.*

naughty
mischievous
disobedient
badly-behaved

***Naughty** Timmy ran away and hid at bath time.*

bad

harmful
damaging

*Smoking is **harmful** to your health.*

rotten
foul
spoiled

*That apple's **rotten**. Throw it away.*

wicked
evil
sinister

*The **wicked** witch turned the prince into a toad.*

nasty
unpleasant
objectionable
offensive

*There's a **nasty** smell coming from that factory.*

faulty
defective
broken

*The tire went flat because of a **faulty** valve.*

poor
crummy
second-rate
shoddy

*The plumber did such a **poor** job that the sink's still blocked.*

bad

miserable
unhappy

*I had a **miserable** time today. Everyone was mean to me.*

severe
serious
disastrous
intense

*The ship was wrecked in a **severe** storm.*

more words that mean bad

awful
atrocious
disgraceful
dreadful
frightful
horrible
shocking
terrible
vile

attractive
lovely
pretty
handsome
good-looking

*You look so **attractive** when you smile.*

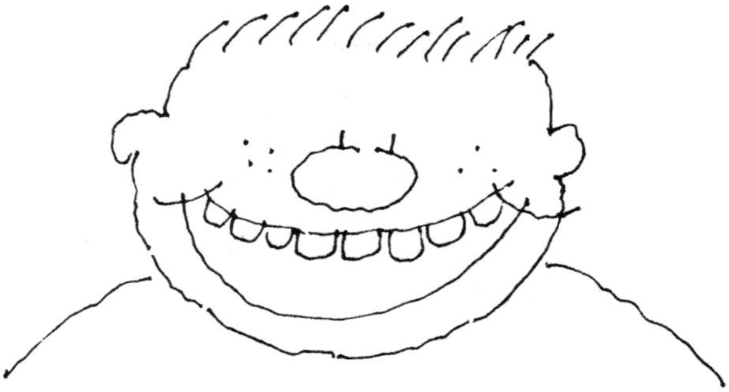

beautiful

cute
sweet

*The ducklings look so **cute** swimming behind their mother.*

elegant
glamorous

*The magazine has pictures of **elegant** models dressed in the latest fashion.*

gorgeous
splendid
glorious
exquisite

*The golden crown was studded with **gorgeous** jewels.*

grown-up
adult
mature
fully-grown

I have one little sister and two ***grown-up*** *brothers.*

huge
great
large
enormous
mighty
giant
gigantic
colossal

As we got closer, we could see how ***huge*** *the CN Tower is.*

big

heavy
bulky
weighty

This parcel is too ***heavy*** *for me to carry.*

vast
huge
extensive
enormous
immense

The Sahara is a ***vast*** *desert.*

handle
like
robin's
eggs

brave
fearless
heroic
courageous

*It was **brave** of Helen to jump into the surf and save her sister.*

daring
adventurous

*Are you **daring** enough to climb right to the top?*

bold

cheeky
rude
insolent
impudent
impertinent

*If you're **cheeky** to your teacher you'll get into trouble.*

album a book with blank pages where you can keep things like photos, pictures or stamps

atlas a book of maps

diary a book with blank pages for you to write about what happens each day

dictionary a book which has a list of words in alphabetical order. You can use it to find out what a word means, how to spell it and how to say it.

book

encyclopedia a book of facts. It has information about many things.

exercise book a book you can write your schoolwork in

manual a book which tells you how to do something or use something

novel a long story book

textbook a book with the information you need to study a subject at school

thesaurus a book of words arranged in groups which have a similar meaning

burst
pop
explode

*The balloon will **burst** if you sit on it.*

shatter
splinter

*The glass will **shatter** if you drop it on the floor.*

break

crack

*Parrots **crack** open seeds with their strong beaks.*

snap
split

***Snap** the biscuit in two so we can have half each.*

crumble

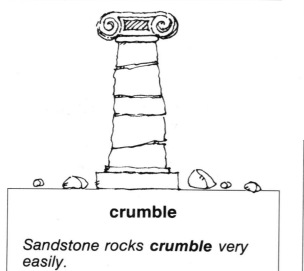

*Sandstone rocks **crumble** very easily.*

wreck
ruin
smash
destroy

*Whenever they come to play they **wreck** all my toys.*

disobey

*You'll be in trouble if you **disobey** the rules.*

intermission

*The lights come on at **intermission** at the movies.*

break

fracture
crack

*You can see where the **fracture** is in the X-ray.*

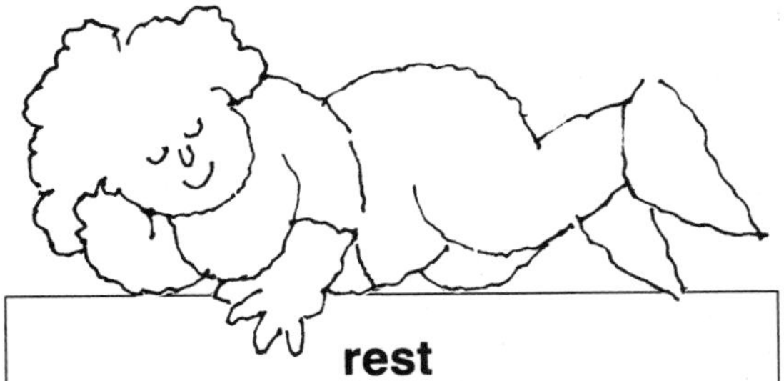

rest
spell

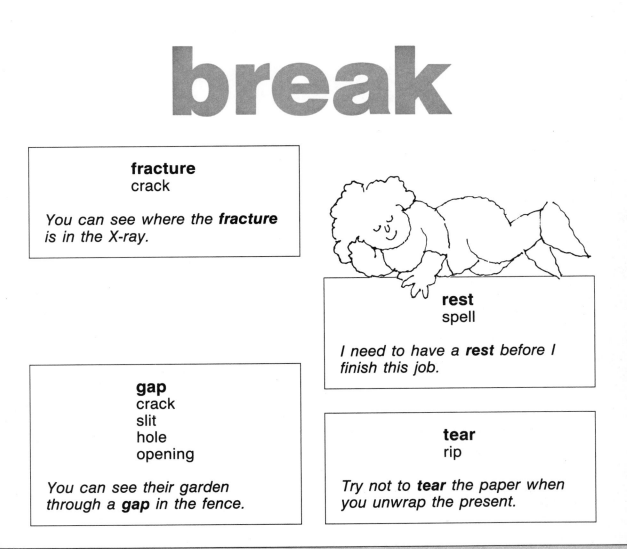

*I need to have a **rest** before I finish this job.*

gap
crack
slit
hole
opening

*You can see their garden through a **gap** in the fence.*

tear
rip

*Try not to **tear** the paper when you unwrap the present.*

colorful or **colourful**
vivid
brilliant
gaudy

Parakeets have ***colourful*** *feathers.*

lively
alert
wide-awake

I'm surprised you're so ***lively*** *after such a late night.*

bright

dazzling
blinding
glaring

The ***dazzling*** *sunshine hurt our eyes.*

shiny
shining
gleaming
glistening
glittering

Here's a ***shiny*** *new dollar coin.*

happy
cheerful
cheery
merry
carefree

They set off down the road singing a ***happy*** *song.*

sunny
clear
cloudless

It's good to see a ***sunny*** *day after so much rain.*

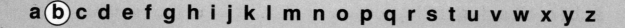

name
christen
nickname

*We'll **name** the dog ''Bluey.''*

send for
summon
fetch

*I think you'd better **send for** the doctor.*

call

phone
telephone

*You can **phone** Hannah and ask her over if you like.*

shout
cry
yell
holler

*Quick! **Shout** for help.*

forgetful
scatterbrained

*She's so **forgetful**, she's always losing things.*

careless

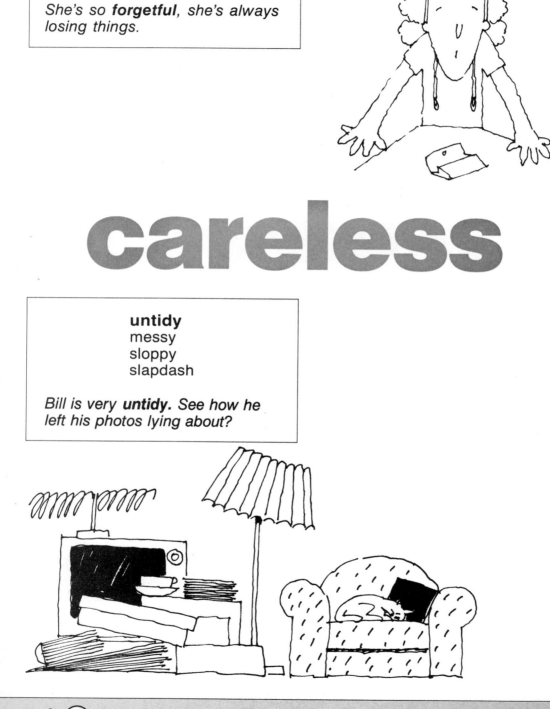

untidy
messy
sloppy
slapdash

*Bill is very **untidy.** See how he left his photos lying about?*

bring

*Pipes **bring** gas to the houses.*

take
move
shift
transport
convey

*Trucks **take** goods from factories to stores.*

carry

support
bear

*Will the ladder **support** your weight?*

capture
arrest

The police set out to ***capture*** *the thief.*

fool
trick
trap
con

You can't ***fool*** *me with a trick like that.*

catch

come down with
develop

Change your wet clothes or you'll ***come down with*** *a cold.*

hear
make out

Did you ***hear*** *what the announcer said?*

find
come upon
surprise
discover
detect

If they ***find*** *us here we'll be in trouble.*

seize
grab
grasp
snatch

We saw the eagle ***seize*** *the rabbit in its claws.*

adjust
vary

*You can **adjust** the colour on the TV set with this knob.*

reorganize
remodel
modify

*We'll have to **reorganize** the room if we want to fit another bed in.*

change

alter
revise
amend

*I think I'll **alter** my story to give it a different ending.*

switch
transfer

*We had to **switch** from the train to a bus because the train track was being fixed.*

exchange
swap
replace

*I'll take the shorts back and **exchange** them for some bigger ones.*

turn
convert
transform

*Do you have any of those toy cars that **turn** into robots?*

different ways to clean things

sweep
brush
mop
polish
dust
vacuum
scour
scrub

clean

spotless
sparkling
clean as a whistle

We polished the car until it was ***spotless****.*

wash
rinse
sponge
bathe

Wash *your hands before dinner.*

empty
bare

*The shelves are **empty** now, ready to be painted.*

obvious
plain
evident

*"Hmm," said the doctor. "It's **obvious** you have the measles."*

clear

fine
sunny
bright
cloudless

*The day was **fine** after the wind blew away the clouds.*

simple
uncomplicated
straightforward

*You should be able to answer this **simple** question.*

transparent
see-through

*I covered the books with **transparent** plastic.*

bright
brainy
smart
intelligent
sharp
quick
brilliant

*She's so **bright** she always gets top marks.*

skilful
skilled
expert
gifted
talented

*She's a **skilful** artist.*

clever

cunning
crafty
shrewd

*They thought up a **cunning** plan of escape.*

mount
ascend

I like to ***mount*** *stairs two at a time.*

scramble
clamber

The children began to ***scramble*** *down the steep hill to the beach.*

climb

scale

The climbers needed ropes to ***scale*** *the steepest part of the mountain.*

cool
fresh
crisp
nippy

*The weather turns **cool** in autumn.*

wintry
chilly
raw
sharp

*A **wintry** wind whistled round the house.*

cold

freezing
icy
frosty
frozen

*Turn on the heater. It's **freezing** in here.*

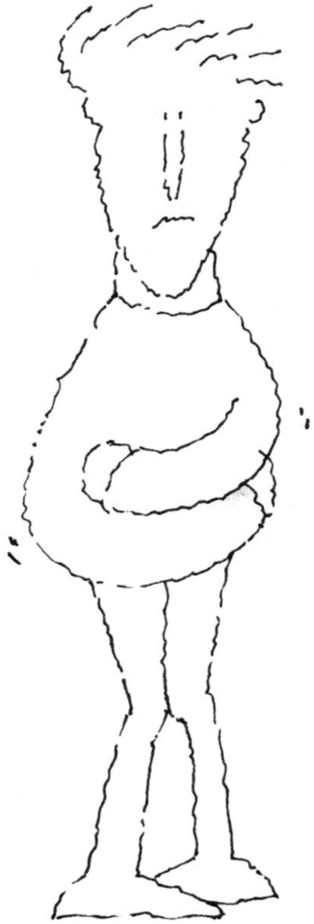

appear

*You'll know the water's boiling when bubbles **appear**.*

happen
occur
take place

*My birthday won't **happen** again until next year.*

come

approach
draw near

*We waved as we saw the boat **approach**.*

visit

*Grandma and Grandpa usually **visit** on Sundays.*

arrive
turn up
show up

*I hope they **arrive** in time for dinner.*

bake to cook something in an oven

barbecue to cook meat, sausages and other food over a fire outside.

boil to heat water or soup until it bubbles and steam comes off. You can also boil eggs and other food by putting them in boiling water.

fry to cook food in a pan using fat or oil

cook

grill to cook food on metal bars that you put under or over a flame

roast this word means nearly the same as **bake** but is mostly used about meat

stew to cook meat and vegetables very slowly in hot soupy liquid

toast to grill bread, muffins or sandwiches

fake
forgery
imitation

*This gem looks like a real diamond but it's only a **fake**.*

model
replica

*The museum had a **model** of a dinosaur.*

copy

impersonate

*Actors often **impersonate** famous people.*

photocopy
duplicate

*Will you **photocopy** this drawing so I can take it home?*

mimic
imitate

*Can you **mimic** the call of a loon?*

trace

***Trace** the map of Australia from your atlas.*

carve

*Sculptors **carve** figures out of stone or wood.*

chop
split

***Chop** the wood for the fire.*

hack
slash

*They had to **hack** their way through the vines to clear a path through the bush.*

cut

clip
snip

***Clip** the picture out of the magazine.*

gash

*Be careful you don't **gash** your foot on the broken glass.*

mow

*I **mow** the lawn to earn pocket money.*

nick
scrape

*It's easy to **nick** yourself when you shave with a razor blade.*

prune
trim

***Prune** the hedge so it doesn't grow too tall.*

cut

saw

***Saw** that piece of timber to the right size.*

slice

*Use a sharp knife to **slice** the bread.*

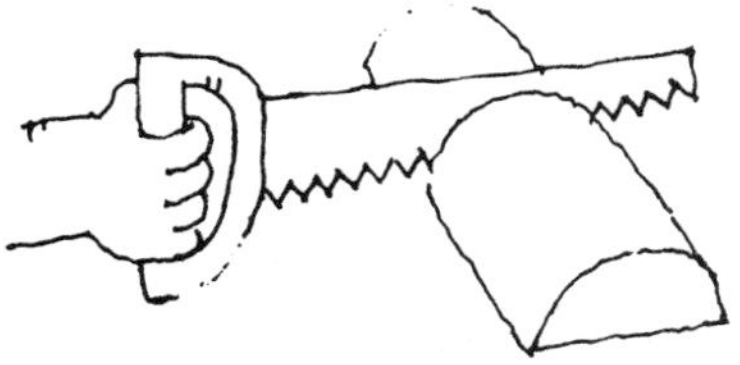

slit

***Slit** the envelope open with a knife.*

shear

*Farmers **shear** wool from their sheep and sell it.*

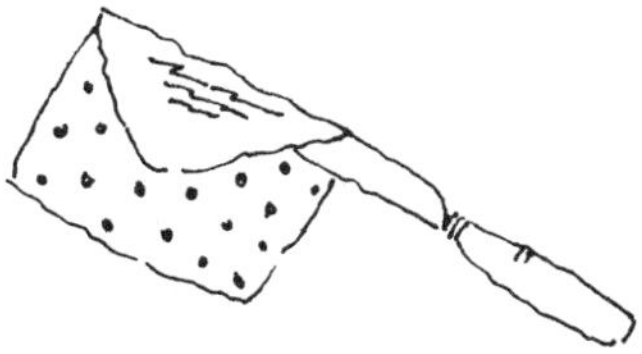

spoil
mess up

*Wear an apron so the paint doesn't **spoil** your clothes.*

damage

vandalize
deface

*People who **vandalize** trains will end up in trouble with the police.*

wreck
destroy
ruin
demolish
smash

*Watch out! If you run into that tree you'll **wreck** your bike.*

filthy
grimy
dusty
greasy
grubby
muddy

*The windows are so **filthy** you can't see outside.*

dirty

messy
untidy
like a pig sty

*Your room is **messy**. Go and clean it up.*

polluted
foul

*The river was so **polluted** all the fish died.*

hate
can't stand
can't bear
object to
loathe
detest

*I **hate** having to eat pumpkin.*

resent

*Robert **resents** anyone who bosses him around.*

dislike

look down on
despise
scorn

*Don't **look down on** people just because they look different.*

bother
interrupt
pester
hassle

*Don't **bother** Grandpa while he's having a rest.*

upset
worry
trouble
distress

*Try not to let their teasing **upset** you.*

disturb

move
shift
meddle with
interfere with

*Don't **move** my painting until it dries.*

be enough
be sufficient

*Will $10 **be enough**?*

get along
fare

*I didn't **get along** so well at the dentist. I had to have two fillings.*

do

finish
complete

*You can go out to play after you **finish** your homework.*

learn
study

*I'm going to **learn** music next year.*

manage
deal with
cope with
handle

*I can't **manage** these hard math problems.*

play

*You can **play** either tennis or hockey on sports day.*

do

perform

*The doctor said they might need to **perform** an operation.*

3

travel at

*Racing cars can **travel at** 300 kilometres per hour.*

gulp

*We had a race to see who could **gulp** down a glass of water first.*

sip

*If I **sip** my lemonade it will last longer.*

guzzle

*If they **guzzle** all that beer they'll be drunk.*

drink

lap

*Our kittens have just learned how to **lap** milk from a saucer.*

slurp

*Some people make loud noises as they **slurp** their soup.*

suck

*Hummingbirds use their long beaks to **suck** nectar from flowers.*

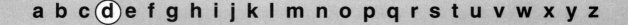

arid
parched
sunbaked

*Few plants can grow in this **arid** land.*

wither
shrivel

*The strong sun will **wither** the plants.*

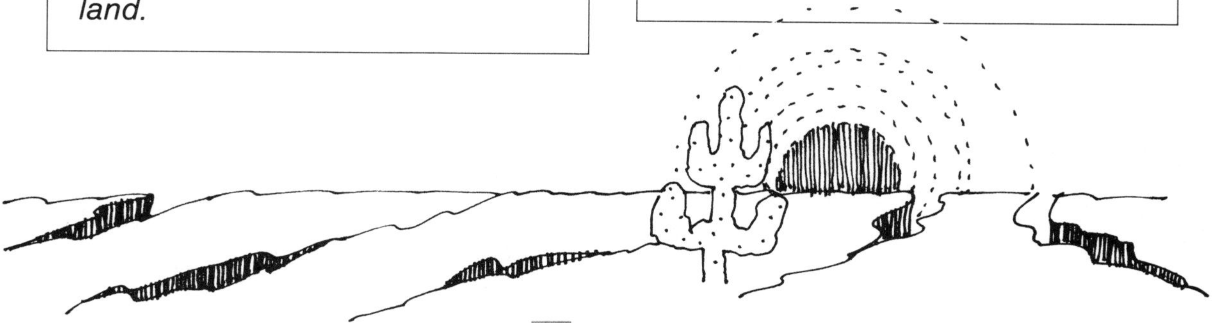

dry

bone-dry

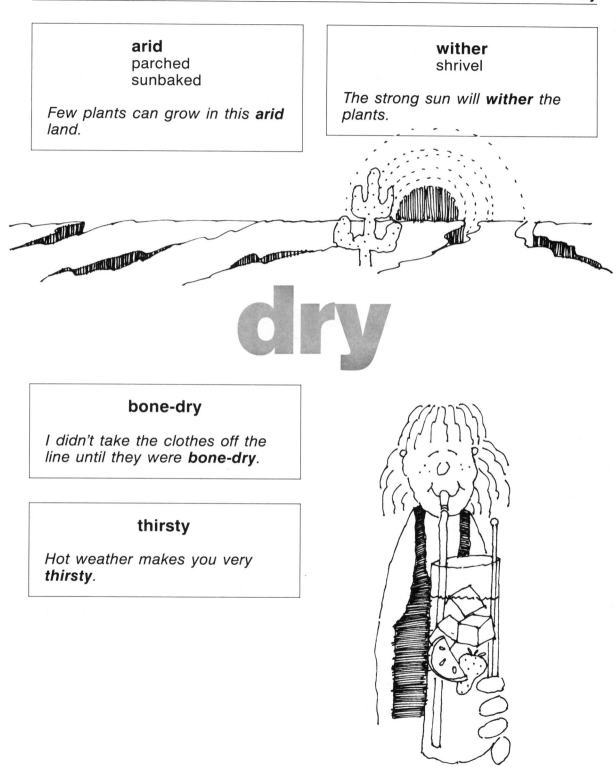

*I didn't take the clothes off the line until they were **bone-dry**.*

thirsty

*Hot weather makes you very **thirsty**.*

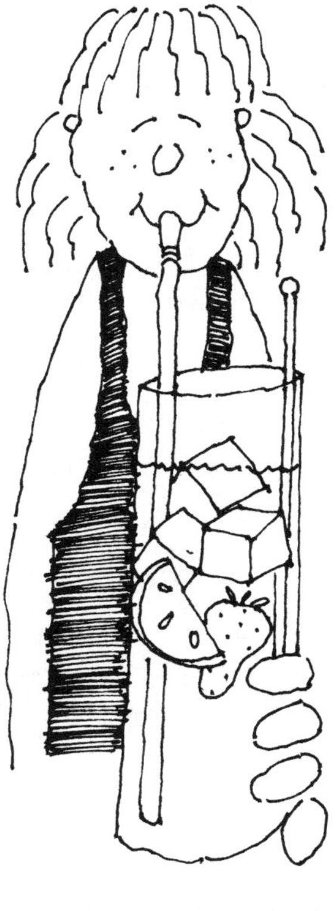

blunt

*The knife is too **blunt** to cut the meat.*

dreary
miserable
gloomy
drab
dismal

*The city looks **dreary** on a cold wet day.*

dull

boring
uninteresting
monotonous
tedious

*Sitting in the car on a long trip can be very **boring**.*

cloudy
overcast
grey

*The sky became **cloudy** and it began to rain.*

flat

*Do you want to use **flat** paint or shiny paint on the walls?*

chew
munch

*Celery makes a loud crunching sound when you **chew** it.*

gobble
wolf down

*There was only just enough time to **gobble** a quick sandwich.*

devour

*Hundreds of ants came to **devour** the dead lizard.*

graze

*We put the cows out to **graze** after we milked them.*

eat

dine

*They were invited to **dine** at the best restaurant in town.*

nibble

*Guinea pigs like to **nibble** lettuce leaves.*

feed on

*Spiders **feed on** small insects that they trap in their webs.*

taste

***Taste** the soup to see if there's enough salt in it.*

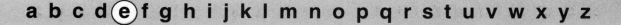

bare

*We'll hang some pictures to brighten up the **bare** walls.*

drain

***Drain** the bath when you've finished.*

empty

blank

*This book has **blank** pages for drawing and lined pages for writing.*

hungry

*I always feel **hungry** when I get home from school.*

clear out

*We have to **clear out** our desks on the last day of school.*

vacant
deserted
uninhabited
unoccupied

*The house next door has been **vacant** for six months.*

complete
conclude
finalize
settle

*We need to **complete** the plans for the concert before tomorrow.*

finish
stop
close
break up

*School will **finish** a week before Christmas.*

end

ending
conclusion

*The book had a sad **ending**.*

finale

*All the actors came on stage for the **finale**.*

result
outcome

*I have no idea what the **result** of the match will be.*

tip

*I jammed the **tip** of my finger in the door.*

average
all right
satisfactory
not bad
passable

*The school report said my work was **average**.*

carnival
show
festival
fete
exhibition
mardi gras

*The school **carnival** raised enough money to build a swimming pool.*

fair

blond
light
pale

*He has very **blond** hair.*

right
just
reasonable

*It isn't **right** for you to have more turns than the others.*

crash
collapse
crumple

*We watched the building **crash** to the ground.*

drop
lessen
decrease

*Let's fly our kites now because the wind might **drop** soon.*

fall

descend
dip

*We saw the plane **descend** suddenly below the clouds.*

sink
plunge

*If too many people get into the boat it will **sink** to the bottom.*

drop
descent

*It's a long **drop** to the bottom of the cliff.*

trip
stumble
slip
tumble
topple over

*Mind you don't **trip** on the stairs.*

brisk
lively
hurried

*We went for a **brisk** walk.*

quick
swift
rapid
speedy

*She's a very **quick** worker and usually finishes first.*

fast

quickly
speedily
swiftly
rapidly
like a flash
like lightning

*The news spread **quickly**.*

express
high-speed

*The **express** train takes only five hours to get from Toronto to Montréal.*

tightly
firmly
securely

*Tie the boat **tightly** to the pier.*

believe
know

*I **believe** you're making a dreadful mistake.*

sense

*I could **sense** that he was really angry.*

feel

experience
notice
be aware of

*You'll only **experience** a small pin-prick when you have the injection.*

touch

*Come and **touch** the furry leaves on this plant.*

seem

*It's so cold today, it makes it **seem** like winter.*

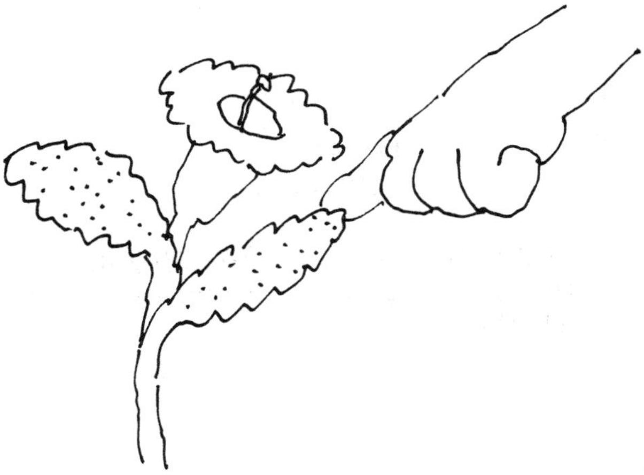

argue
quarrel
squabble
have a row
bicker

*My brothers always **argue** over football.*

match
wrestling match
boxing match

*The Hulk clashes with The Bruiser in the **match** tonight.*

fight

battle
raid
attack
assault
war

*Two thousand soldiers were killed in the **battle**.*

quarrel
argument
disagreement
squabble
row

*My sister and I had a **quarrel** over who should do the washing-up.*

brawl
scuffle
free-for-all

*There was a nasty **brawl** at the football game.*

resist
oppose

*Our cats always **resist** our attempts to put them outside at night.*

discover
come across
come upon

*No one will ever **discover** our hiding place.*

find

learn
realize
discover

*When they **learn** that our teacher is my uncle they will be surprised.*

see
notice
observe
spot
detect

*If you look hard, you might **see** where the crow has its nest.*

trace
track down
locate

*The police are trying to **trace** the thief.*

work out
figure out
come up with

*Did you **work out** the answer to the question?*

cure
heal

*This medicine will **cure** your sore throat.*

solve
deal with

*Lights will **solve** the traffic problem at this corner.*

fix

mend
repair
patch

*We are going to **mend** the hole in the fence.*

drip
trickle
dribble

We could feel the rain ***drip*** *down our legs and into our shoes.*

pour
stream
drain
surge

Storm water will ***pour*** *down the gutters after heavy rain.*

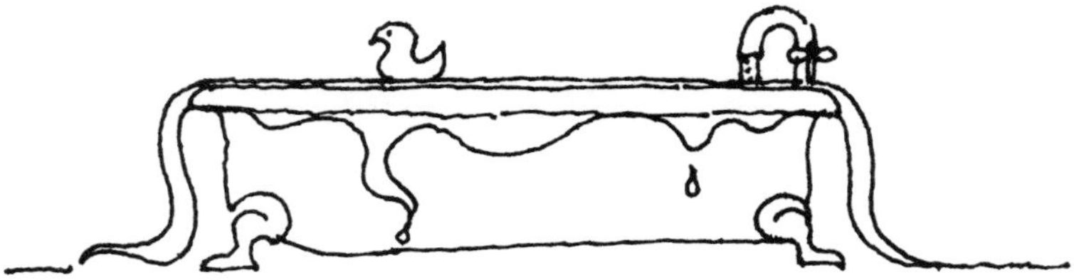

flow

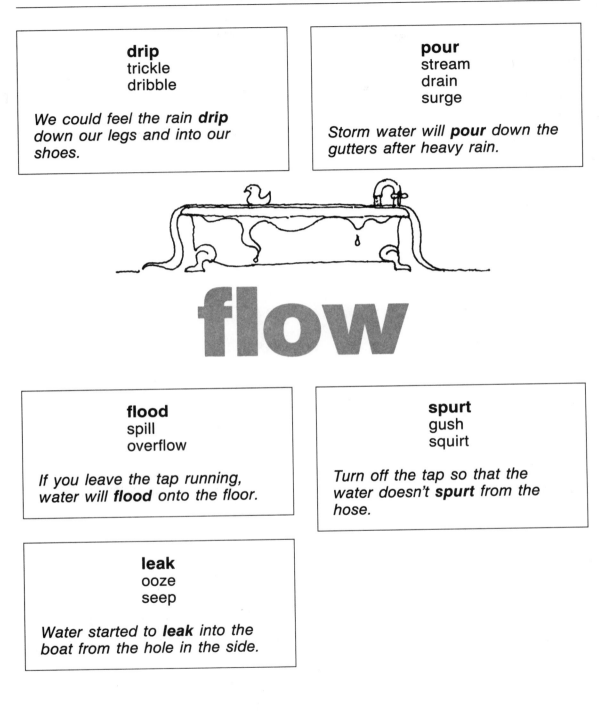

flood
spill
overflow

If you leave the tap running, water will ***flood*** *onto the floor.*

spurt
gush
squirt

Turn off the tap so that the water doesn't ***spurt*** *from the hose.*

leak
ooze
seep

Water started to ***leak*** *into the boat from the hole in the side.*

drift
float
stream

*As clouds **drift** across the sun they make shadows on the ground.*

pilot

*Captain Morris can **pilot** any kind of airplane.*

fly

flutter
flit

*Look at the butterfly **flutter** by.*

go by air
go by plane

*We will **go by air** to Fiji for our holidays.*

soar
glide
flap
hover
swoop

*We watched the bird **soar** high above the trees.*

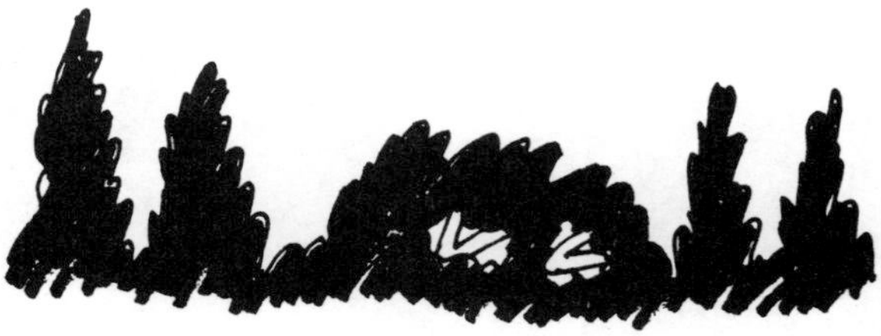

chase
hunt
pursue
track
tail
shadow

*The police jumped into their cars to **chase** the bank robbers.*

copy
imitate

***Copy** me if you want to learn this dance.*

follow

come after

*Floods often **come after** heavy rain.*

understand
work out
catch on to
make head or tail of

*He speaks so softly I can't **understand** what he is saying.*

bully
terrorize
intimidate

*I won't let the big kids **bully** you into giving up the swing.*

startle
alarm
shock

*If you move too quickly you'll **startle** the horses.*

frighten

scare
terrify
make your hair stand on end
make your blood run cold
make your flesh creep

*Ghost stories **scare** me and give me bad dreams.*

nervous
anxious
worried
jittery

*She was very **nervous** about singing in front of the whole school.*

timid
fearful

*Sam was too **timid** to pat the dog.*

frightened

scared
afraid
scared stiff
scared to death
terrified
petrified
panic-stricken

*They were **scared** when they had to spend the night in the spooky cave.*

complete
whole
entire

*There are 52 playing cards in a **complete** pack.*

taken
occupied

*The seats in the bus were all **taken** so we had to stand up.*

full

packed
crowded
crammed
jammed
brimming
overflowing
bulging
bursting at the seams

*The cupboard is **packed** with books and toys.*

humorous
amusing
ridiculous
comical
hilarious
witty

*Her **humorous** story about her puppy made us all laugh.*

funny

strange
odd
queer
peculiar
weird
unusual
curious

*The cake tasted **strange** because I used salt instead of sugar by mistake.*

earn
obtain

I want to ***earn*** *some money by doing jobs after school.*

prepare
make
fix

I usually ***prepare*** *my own breakfast.*

get

fetch
bring
gather
collect
pick up

It's my job to ***fetch*** *the letters from the letter box.*

receive

Did you ***receive*** *an invitation to the party?*

win
gain

The best painting will ***win*** *the prize.*

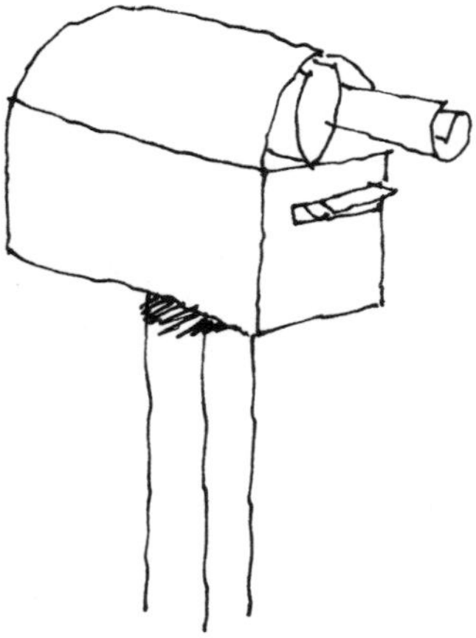

arrive
come
reach

When did you ***arrive*** *here?*

contact
reach

I phoned his house but I couldn't ***contact*** *him.*

get

become
grow

The weather announcer said the wind will ***become*** *stronger.*

understand

Why didn't you laugh? Didn't you ***understand*** *the joke?*

donate
contribute
give away
make a present of

*Will you please **donate** some money to the children's hospital?*

offer

*Look at Spot! He wants to **offer** you his ball.*

give

hand over
turn over

*"Come on," he snarled, "**hand over** the money or I'll shoot."*

present
award

*The president of the football club will **present** a silver trophy to the winning team.*

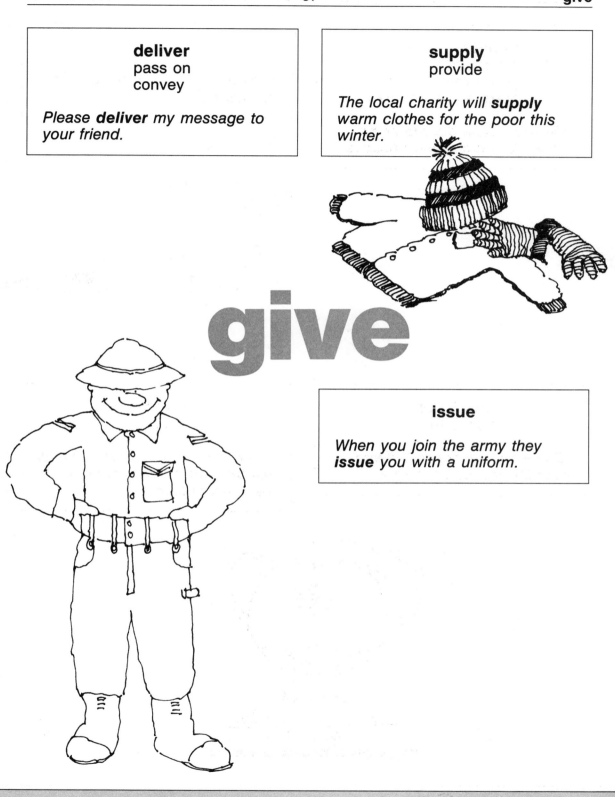

deliver
pass on
convey

*Please **deliver** my message to your friend.*

supply
provide

*The local charity will **supply** warm clothes for the poor this winter.*

give

issue

*When you join the army they **issue** you with a uniform.*

escape
flee
sneak away
run away

*The prisoners saw their chance to **escape** while the guard was asleep.*

return

*I have to **return** home before dark.*

go

leave
depart
set off
clear out

*I have to **leave** in the morning.*

vanish
disappear

*We watched the sun **vanish** behind a cloud.*

retreat
back

*The savage dog forced them to **retreat** into a corner.*

become
grow
turn
get

*Our faces **become** red when we're hot.*

continue
stretch
extend
reach
spread

*The mountains **continue** far into the distance.*

go

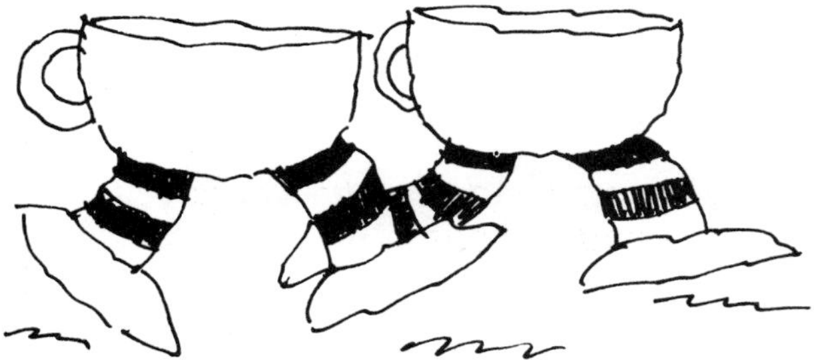

travel
journey
roam
wander

*We are going to **travel** down the Fraser River in the holidays.*

belong
fit

*Where do the cups **belong**?*

clever
bright
smart

*I'm not as **clever** at mathematics as you, but I'm better at reading.*

loyal
true
reliable
dependable
devoted

***Loyal** friends always stick up for their pals.*

good

kind
nice
helpful
thoughtful
considerate

*It was **kind** of you to drive me home when it was raining.*

skilled
skilful
expert
able
experienced
capable

*We need a **skilled** mechanic to fix the car.*

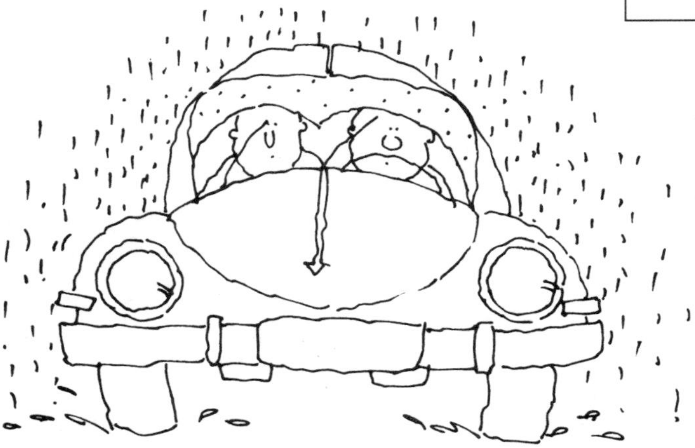

excellent
wonderful
marvellous
top
first-class
outstanding
exceptional

*A lifesaver must be an **excellent** swimmer.*

pleasant
enjoyable
welcome
agreeable

*We had a **pleasant** day walking in the mountains.*

good

interesting
exciting
entertaining
fascinating
gripping
thrilling

*They showed an **interesting** film on space travel.*

well-behaved
well-mannered
polite
as good as gold
courteous

*The children were **well-behaved** on the long bus trip.*

There are more words like **good** on the next two pages.

healthy
wholesome

*Eat **healthy** food if you want to grow big and strong.*

valuable
expensive
precious
costly

*Dad's cross because I left his **valuable** tools out in the rain.*

good

perfect
fine
undamaged
unspoiled
immaculate
the very best

*I've had my bike for three years and it's still in **perfect** condition.*

more words that mean good

- admirable
- amazing
- choice
- cool
- fabulous
- fine
- first-rate
- great
- hot
- sensational
- splendid
- super
- superb
- terrific

useful
handy
helpful

*A dictionary is a **useful** book to have nearby when you are reading or writing.*

good

suitable
convenient

*Would Friday be a **suitable** day to come over?*

How about Friday?

batch

The last ***batch*** *of muffins is ready to go into the oven.*

gather
collect
assemble
cluster

Lots of people usually ***gather*** *to watch the seals being fed.*

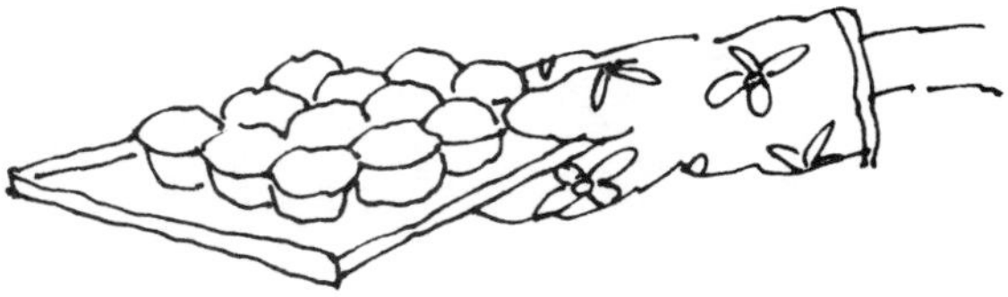

group

bundle
bunch
clump

Gather the sticks into a ***bundle*** *for the fire.*

set
pack
collection

I need two more cards to make a whole ***set****.*

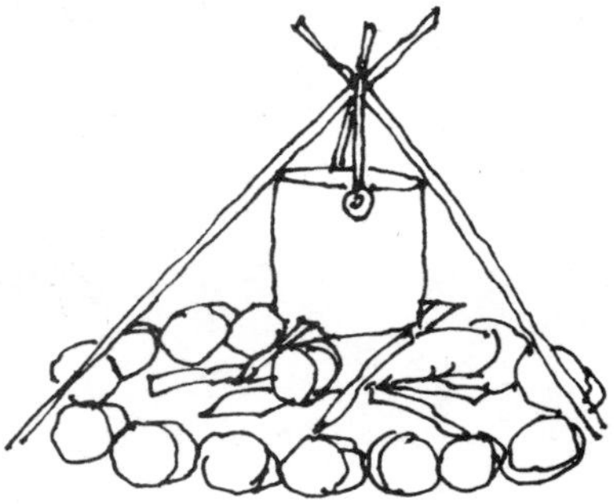

sort
arrange
organize

I have to ***sort*** *the stamps before I put them in my album.*

club
society
association

*Do you belong to a secret **club**?*

section
branch
division
part

*Our school has a junior **section** and a primary **section**.*

group

crowd
mob
throng
gang

*There was a noisy **crowd** at the café.*

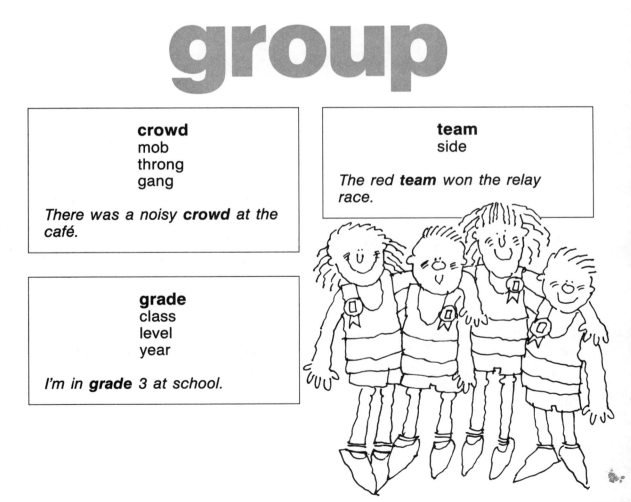

grade
class
level
year

*I'm in **grade** 3 at school.*

team
side

*The red **team** won the relay race.*

dangle
trail
swing
droop

*Thick vines **dangle** from the trees in rainforests.*

be suspended

*A model airplane can **be suspended** from the ceiling.*

hang

drape

*Sometimes we **drape** blankets over the table and make a cubbyhole underneath.*

pin
nail
tack

***Pin** the posters on the wall.*

cheerful
merry
bright
jolly
joyful
carefree
light-hearted

These books and toys will help make your stay in hospital more ***cheerful****.*

glad
pleased

I'm really ***glad*** *you came.*

happy

delighted
thrilled
overjoyed

Tom and Lee were ***delighted*** *with their birthday presents.*

satisfied
content

I hope you're ***satisfied*** *with your new jeans.*

difficult
tricky
awkward
complicated

*This puzzle is too **difficult** for me to work out.*

stiff
rigid

*The **stiff** cardboard box didn't bend when I sat on it.*

hard

firm
solid
set

*I like boiled eggs to be **firm** in the centre.*

unpleasant
awful

*My cousins had an **unpleasant** journey through the snowstorm.*

carefully
closely
intently

*If you look **carefully** you can see the fine lines on your finger tips.*

tiring
exhausting

*Mother said she'd had a **tiring** day at work.*

hard

tough
chewy

*Meat gets **tough** if you cook it too long.*

strong
forceful
powerful

*If the door sticks, just give it a **strong** push.*

consist of
be made up of

*A soccer team should **consist of** 11 players.*

keep
put
place

*I think we should **keep** the desk near the window.*

have

contain

*All the rooms **contain** 35 desks.*

own
possess

*Does your class **own** a computer?*

allow
stand
put up with
tolerate

*You're making too much noise. I won't **allow** it.*

give birth to
produce

*Cats **give birth to** kittens.*

have

experience
go through

*If we **experience** rough seas I'll probably be sick.*

need
ought
should
must

*I feel sick and I **need** to lie down.*

aid
assistance
support

*The Red Cross gives **aid** to people in trouble.*

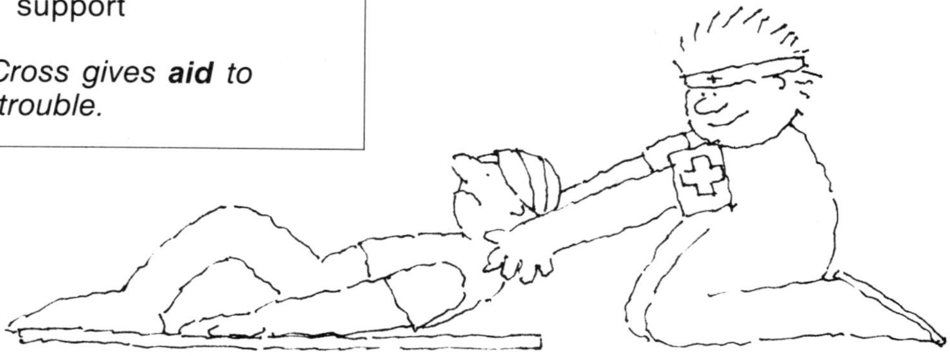

help

improve
make better

*The doctor said glasses would **improve** my eyesight.*

lend a hand
give a hand

*Will you **lend a hand** to move this cupboard.*

serve

*I asked the man behind the counter to **serve** me.*

bury
stash

*Pirates used to **bury** treasure in caves.*

cover up
block out
blot out

*Dark clouds began to **cover up** the sun.*

hide

camouflage

*Wear brown and green clothes if you want to **camouflage** yourself in the forest.*

disguise

*He wanted to **disguise** his bald head with a wig.*

conceal

*It was easy for the magician to **conceal** the card in her sleeve.*

keep secret
hush up

*We managed to **keep** Kim's surprise gift **secret** until the day of her birthday.*

beat
thrash
whip
flog

*They used to **beat** convicts when they did something wrong.*

smack
slap
spank
whack
belt
wallop

*Paul ducked out of the way before she had a chance to **smack** him on the bottom.*

hit

punch
clout
sock
slug
clobber

*He said he'd **punch** me if I told on him.*

strike

***Strike** the ball with the middle of the bat.*

tap
touch

*You're out if I **tap** you on the arm.*

bump
knock

I'm sorry. I didn't mean to ***bump*** *you.*

crash into
smash into
bump into
collide with

We saw the car ***crash into*** *the brick wall.*

hit

thump
bang
pound
bash
hammer

His face went red with anger and he started to ***thump*** *the table.*

blazing
burning
scorching
blistering
baking
fiery
boiling

*Let's sit in the shade, away from the **blazing** sun.*

spicy
peppery

***Spicy** food makes my eyes water.*

hot

feverish
flaming
burning

*When I was sick, my whole body was **feverish**.*

warm
summery
mild

*We often have dinner outside on **warm** evenings.*

lukewarm

***Lukewarm** water is best for the baby's bath.*

apartment a place like a condominium, but usually smaller, which you pay rent to live in

cabin a small house with only two or three rooms

castle a very large house with thick stone walls, often with towers and a moat to keep out an enemy

condominium one of several homes that are all in one large building

house

cottage a small house, often used for vacations

hut a small cabin. It can also be called a **shack**.

mansion a very big or grand house

palace a grand house where a king, queen or other very important person lives

townhouse one of the houses in a row of houses joined together.

ache
throb

*My tooth began to **ache** when I ate the ice cube.*

injure
wound

*People who go hunting with guns have to be careful not to **injure** themselves or anybody else.*

hurt

harm

*Our gentle old dog would never **harm** anyone.*

sting
smart

*If you cut your finger it will **sting**.*

upset
insulted

*I was **upset** when they called me horrible names.*

famous
distinguished
prominent

*She made a speech to welcome the Prime Minister and the other **famous** guests.*

special

*Your birthday is a **special** day for you.*

important

necessary
essential

*Fresh air and exercise are **necessary** for good health.*

valuable
good

*We keep our **valuable** things on shelves where the baby can't reach.*

amazing
fascinating
remarkable
intriguing

*Penguins are **amazing** birds.*

interesting

entertaining
amusing

*Grandma tells us lots of **entertaining** stories about when she was a little girl.*

exciting
thrilling

*Please don't make me go to bed now. This is the most **exciting** part of the movie.*

become a member of
enter
enrol in
sign up with

*Do you have to pay to **become a member of** the club?*

meet
come together

*The shop is on the corner where the two roads **meet**.*

join

link
connect

*A new railway line will **link** the two towns.*

tie
fasten
attach
secure

***Tie** the end of the rope to the branch.*

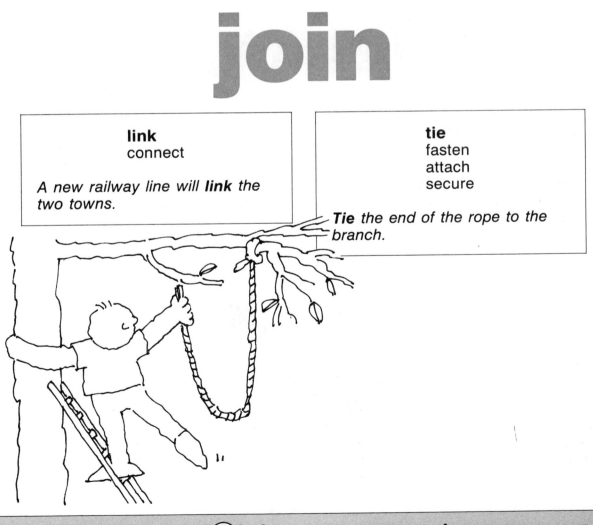

bounce

*Bill can **bounce** higher than anyone on the trampoline.*

dance
skip
hop
prance

*I wish you wouldn't **dance** about while I'm trying to brush your hair.*

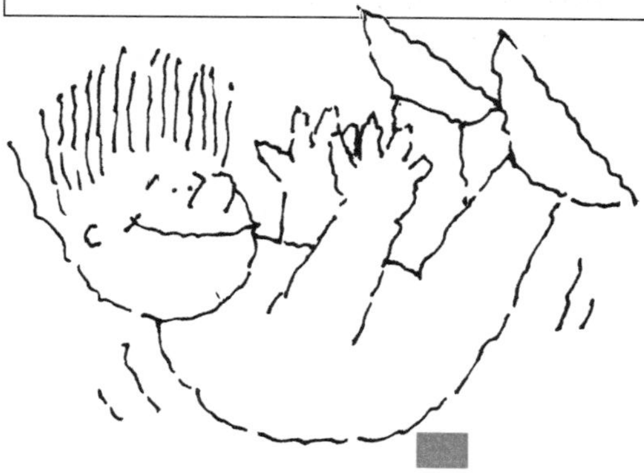

jump

buck
rear

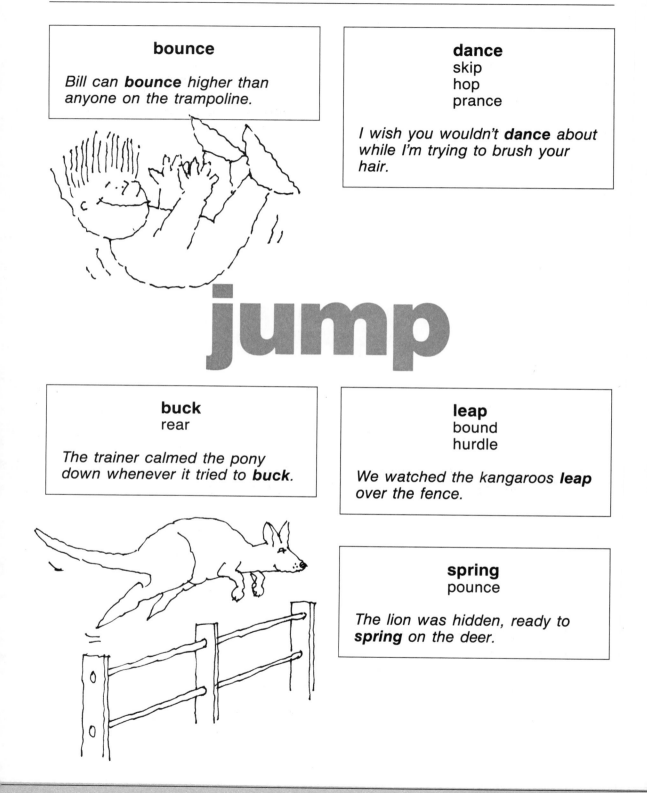

*The trainer calmed the pony down whenever it tried to **buck**.*

leap
bound
hurdle

*We watched the kangaroos **leap** over the fence.*

spring
pounce

*The lion was hidden, ready to **spring** on the deer.*

continue
go on

I'm so tired I can't ***continue*** *walking much further.*

obey
follow
observe

Obey *the rules and you'll stay out of trouble.*

keep

hold
guard
detain

The police decided to ***hold*** *them in jail overnight.*

put
store
stow

There are lockers where you can ***put*** *your bags.*

look after
save
mind

Will you ***look after*** *my seat until I come back?*

be familiar with

After a week of practice we will all ***be familiar with*** *the words of the new song.*

experience
feel

It would be great to ***experience*** *what it's like to live in outer space.*

know

be sure of
be certain of
be confident of

If you want to ***be sure of*** *the meaning of the word, look it up in the dictionary.*

have learned

I ***have learned*** *how to tie a reef knot.*

have met

I ***have met*** *Sally and Tim. They live on my street.*

remember
recall
recollect

I don't ***remember*** *where I left my jumper.*

know

recognize
identify

Would you ***recognize*** *me without my beard?*

understand
see
realize
comprehend

Now I ***understand*** *why she was laughing.*

giggle
chuckle
titter
chortle

*When I made funny faces at my friend she started to **giggle**.*

laugh

roar with laughter
kill yourself laughing
split your sides
crack up

*When the clown's pants fell down it made the audience **roar with laughter**.*

sneer
smirk
snicker

*Don't **sneer** at me. You don't know the answer either.*

abandon
desert

The crew had to ***abandon*** *the sinking ship.*

go out
exit

They had to ***go out*** *by the side door.*

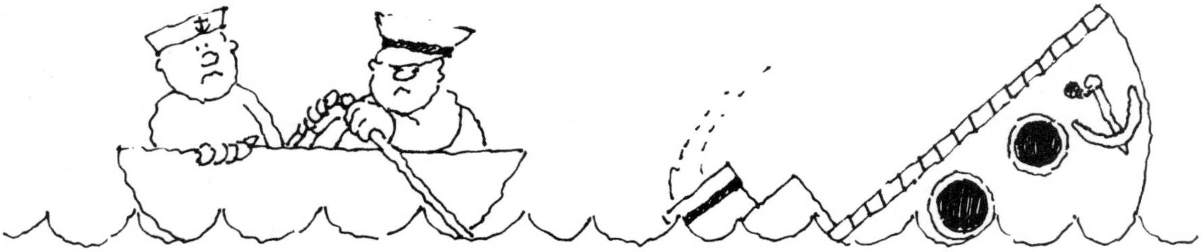

leave

depart

The plane will ***depart*** *for Halifax at 10 o'clock.*

put off
defer

Let's ***put off*** *our homework till after lunch.*

give

Grandpa said he'd ***give*** *me his gold watch in his will.*

quit
resign
retire

Dad doesn't like his job so he's going to ***quit****.*

bright
airy

*The big windows made the room **bright**.*

light as a feather

*What can be in this box? It's as **light as a feather**.*

light

fine
flimsy
delicate

*She wore only a **fine** cotton dress and sandals.*

pale
pastel

*The walls are painted **pale** blue.*

floating
buoyant

***Floating** yellow markers in the river show where to moor the boats.*

catch fire
burn
ignite

The wet wood took a long time to ***catch fire****.*

illuminate

Hundreds of candles were used to ***illuminate*** *the stage.*

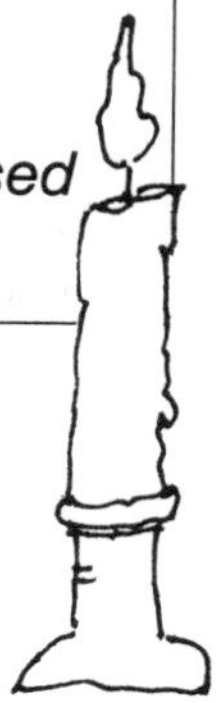

light

Here are some words for what lights do.

burn
flare
flash
flicker
glare
gleam
glimmer
glint
glisten
glitter
glow
shimmer
sparkle
twinkle

admire
respect

*I **admire** people who are brave enough to be astronauts.*

love
adore
be mad about
be crazy about
be fond of
have a soft spot for

*I'm going to be a vet because I know I will always **love** animals.*

like

enjoy

*The film was long and boring so we didn't really **enjoy** it.*

prefer
want
wish for
fancy

*Do you **prefer** plain or flavoured yogurt?*

value
appreciate
treasure
cherish

*Dad lives in Singapore, so I really **value** the time I spend with him when he visits us.*

lonely

homesick
lonesome
unhappy

*He felt very **homesick** on the first night away from his family.*

remote
out-of-the-way
distant
isolated
solitary

*Children who live in **remote** areas have their school lessons by radio and video.*

harsh
raucous

Listen to the ***harsh*** *cries of the crows.*

shrill
piercing
ear-splitting
blaring

I can hear the letter carrier's ***shrill*** *whistle.*

loud

noisy
deafening
thunderous

The hall was filled with ***noisy*** *cheering.*

strong
powerful

A singer needs a ***strong*** *voice.*

YAHOO
HOORAY

clear
audible

*Speak in a **clear** voice so we can all hear you.*

loud

loud sounds

- bang
- blast
- boom
- clamour
- crash
- din
- howl
- racket
- roar
- row
- ruckus
- rumble
- rumpus
- shriek
- thunder
- tumult
- uproar

BANG

assemble
manufacture
turn out
put together

*They **assemble** cars at this factory.*

form

*Join hands and **form** a ring.*

make

build
construct
erect
put up

*We're going to **build** a tree house in the maple tree.*

invent
create

*I'm going to **invent** a robot that puts my toys away.*

prepare
fix
get ready

*Whose turn is it to **prepare** dinner?*

add up to
amount to
total

*Two and two **add up to** four.*

force
compel

*I won't eat my spinach, even if you try to **force** me.*

make

cause
produce
bring about

*Too much sun will **cause** sunburn.*

type
sort
kind
style

*What **type** of car is that?*

earn
obtain
get
acquire

*Do you want to **earn** some money by washing the car?*

indicate
show

*Flashing red lights **indicate** danger ahead.*

nasty
spiteful
unkind
cruel

*The **nasty** things they said made me cry.*

mean

intend
plan
aim
propose
have in mind

*What do you **intend** to do now?*

stingy
selfish
greedy
miserly

*He's so **stingy**, he never shares his french fries with anyone.*

blend
combine

*You can **blend** yellow and blue to make green.*

mingle

*The robbers ran out of the bank and tried to **mingle** with the crowds on the street.*

mix

come together
merge

*The two creeks **come together** to form a river.*

jumble
scramble

*I'll **jumble** these letters and you make them into a word.*

shuffle

***Shuffle** the cards before you deal them.*

stir
mash

***Stir** butter and milk into the potatoes.*

go forward
proceed
advance
travel

*If you press the button the robot will **go forward** across the room.*

leave
depart
go away

*I'll miss my friends when I **leave**.*

move

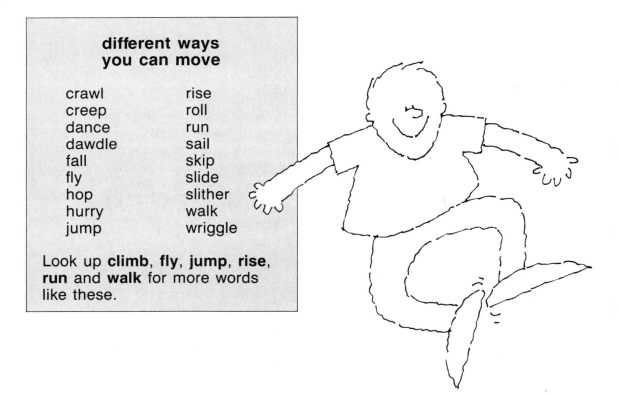

different ways you can move

crawl
creep
dance
dawdle
fall
fly
hop
hurry
jump
rise
roll
run
sail
skip
slide
slither
walk
wriggle

Look up **climb**, **fly**, **jump**, **rise**, **run** and **walk** for more words like these.

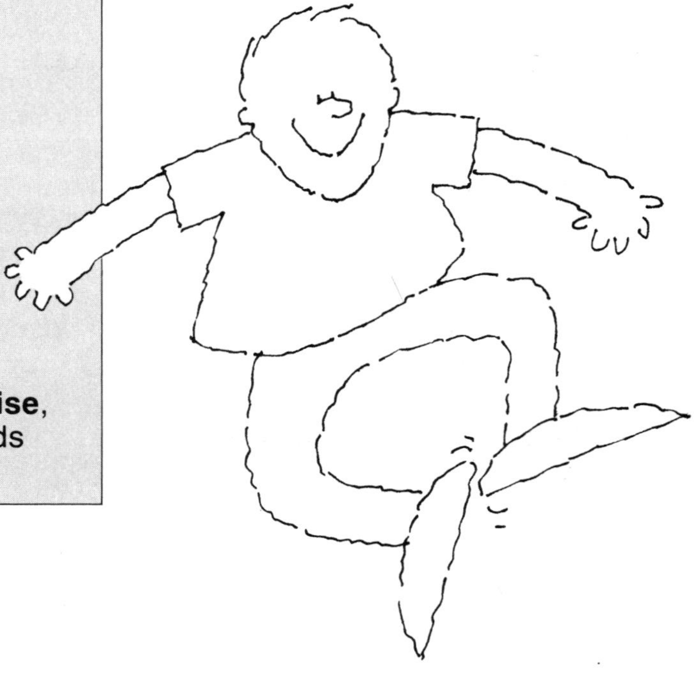

bring
carry
shift

***Bring** your bike in out of the rain.*

remove
take away

*Please **remove** your bag from the chair so I can sit down.*

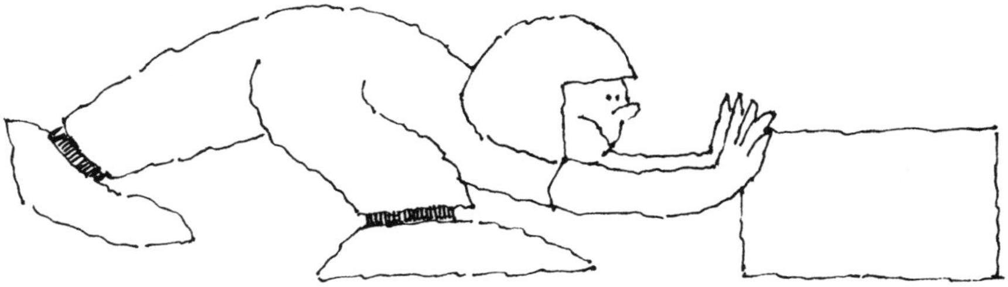

move

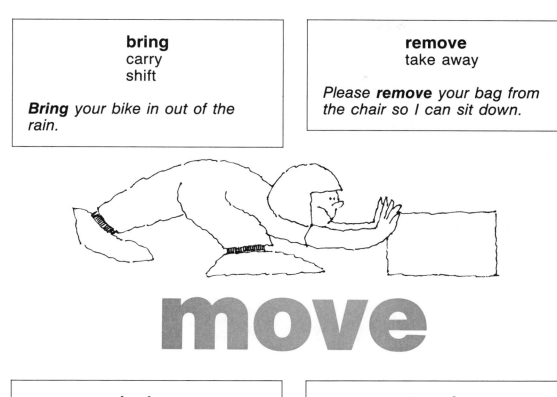

budge
shift
stir

*Sit still and don't **budge** until I come back.*

transfer

*See if you can **transfer** the pancake from the pan to the plate without breaking it.*

bump
push
knock
disturb

*Don't **bump** my model car while the glue's setting.*

different ways you can move things

drop
hit
lift
pull
push
throw

Look up **carry**, **pull**, **push**, **put**, **send**, **shake**, **take**, **throw** and **turn** for more words like these.

attractive
pretty
handsome

*You look very **attractive** when you smile.*

delicious
yummy
tasty
luscious
scrumptious

*Susan's birthday cake was really **delicious**.*

nice

beautiful
lovely
charming
exquisite

*Such a **beautiful** painting must be worth a lot of money.*

stylish
fashionable
elegant
glamorous

*She bought a **stylish** new dress for the party.*

comfortable
cosy

*They live in a **comfortable** house with a big garden.*

enjoyable
delightful
wonderful
glorious

*We had an **enjoyable** holiday.*

friendly
sweet
warm
good-natured

*Everyone was so **friendly**, I had a really good time.*

nice

fine
mild
pleasant

*I hope we have **fine** weather for our picnic.*

kind
good
helpful
thoughtful
generous
considerate

*It's **kind** of you to feed my dogs while I'm away.*

ancient
olden
early
prehistoric

*In **ancient** times, huge dinosaurs roamed the earth.*

old-fashioned
traditional

*We dressed up in **old-fashioned** clothes for our play about Confederation.*

old

antique
vintage

*We have an **antique** sword that is 300 years old.*

elderly
aged

*Great-grandpa lives in a home for **elderly** people.*

last
past
previous
former

*I like my new school, but I still miss my friends at my **last** school.*

old

worn-out
shabby
used
tattered

*I don't want these **worn-out** clothes any more.*

grown-up
big
mature

*Are you **grown-up** enough to go to the store by yourself?*

ask for

I'm going to the cafeteria to ***ask for*** *a roll for lunch.*

demand
insist

You should take the faulty watch back to the shop and ***demand*** *that they give you one that works.*

order

command
instruction

Soldiers have to obey their officers' ***commands****.*

tell
direct
instruct
command

Tell *them to come to the office immediately.*

At once!

arrange
sort
sort out
organize

Arrange *the forks, knives and spoons so they are in separate compartments.*

condition
repair
shape
state

Check to see if the tent is in good ***condition*** *before we go camping.*

order

arrangement
pattern
sequence

Why did you change the ***arrangement*** *of the books on the library shelf?*

choice
selection

*You may have first **choice** of the cookies.*

remove
take

*I had to stop to **remove** the burr from my foot.*

pick

choose
select
decide on

***Choose** the one you want and leave the rest.*

gather
harvest
reap
pluck

*You can usually **gather** mushrooms in the forest.*

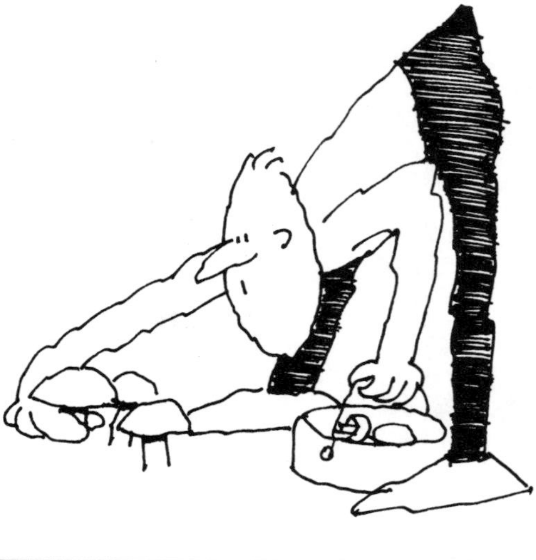

collage a picture made by sticking things like leaves, grass, bits of coloured paper or material onto paper

diagram a drawing or plan of how something works

drawing a picture made with pen or pencil

illustration a picture in a book

mural a picture painted on a wall

picture

painting a picture that you make using paint

pattern a picture of shapes repeated many times over. Wallpaper, carpets and gift wrapping paper have patterns on them.

photo a picture you take with a camera. This word is short for **photograph**.

portrait a picture of a person

poster a large picture you can stick on a wall

sketch a drawing that you do quickly.

bit
scrap
shred

*He tore off a **bit** of paper and wrote his phone number on it.*

flake

***Flakes** of paint were peeling off the walls.*

piece

chip

*This cup has a **chip** out of the side.*

splinter
fragment
sliver

*There's a **splinter** of wood in my finger.*

lump
chunk
hunk

*I hate the sort of soup that has **lumps** of meat floating in it.*

share
helping
portion

*I want to save my **share** of the pie for later.*

piece

part
section

*Just give me the **part** of the paper with the comics in it.*

slice
slab
wedge

*Did you see the huge **slice** of cake he took?*

backlog

*There was a **backlog** of letters waiting to be answered.*

heap
load
mound
mountain
mass

*The truck tipped a **heap** of gravel onto the road.*

pile

collection
hoard

*He bought some more stickers to add to his **collection**.*

stack

*After the party there was a **stack** of dirty plates to be washed.*

drift
bank

*The car skidded off the road and into a deep **drift** of snow.*

clear
obvious

*It was **clear** from the look on her face that she was bored.*

plain

ordinary
everyday

*Their **ordinary** little car looked shabby amongst the big fancy ones.*

unattractive

*A coat of white paint will make the **unattractive** old house look quite smart.*

simple

*I like **simple** food better than strong spicy food.*

drag
haul
lug
heave

*Please help me **drag** this heavy table over to the window.*

tear
wrench

*She tried to **tear** her arm free, but it was held too tightly.*

pull

strain

*Our dogs always **strain** at their leashes when we take them for a walk.*

tug
yank
jerk

*Some fish **tug** so hard on the line you wonder if you've caught a whale!*

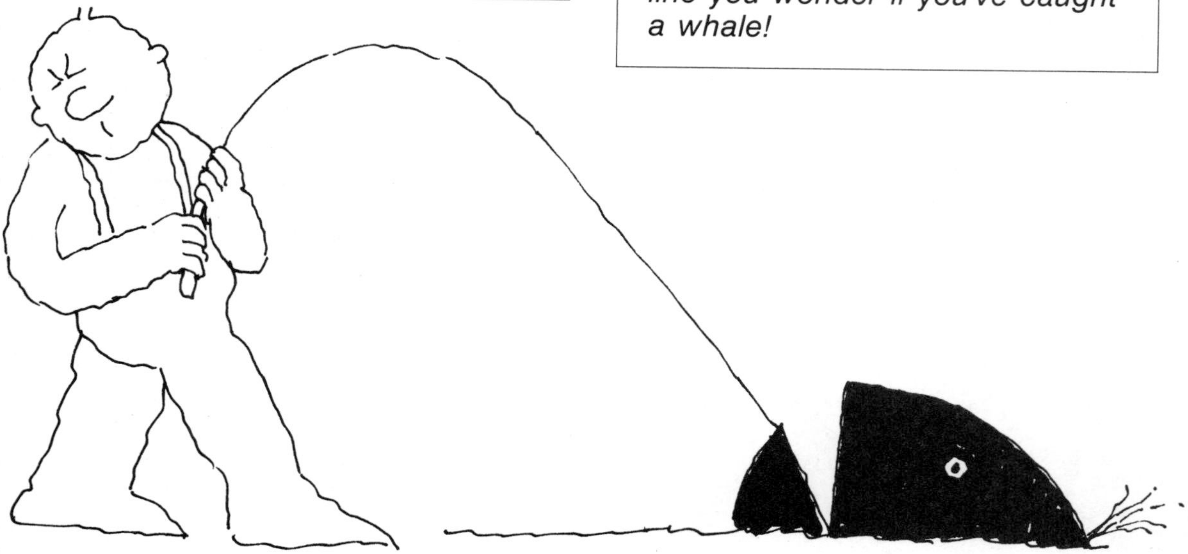

draw

*When I'm cold I climb into bed and **draw** the blankets up over my head.*

tow

*Speed boats can **tow** water-skiers.*

pull

hitch

*You'd better **hitch** up your shorts before they fall down.*

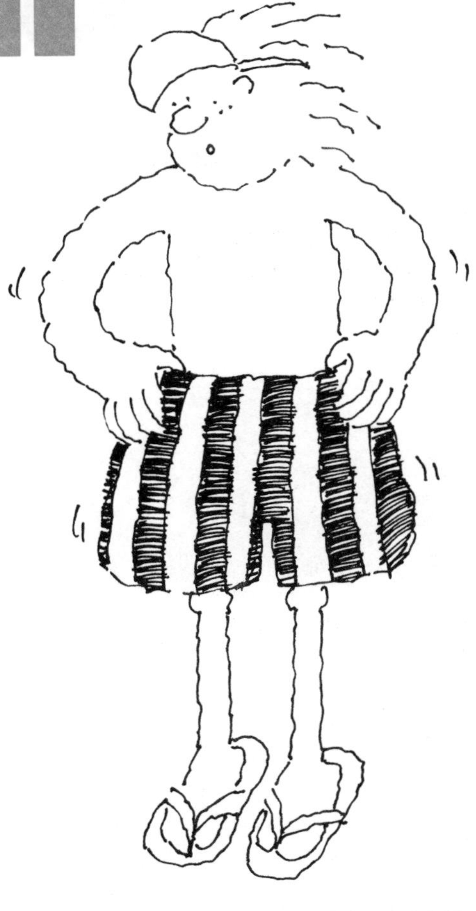

bump
knock
jostle

Dodgem cars ***bump*** *one another as they speed around the ring.*

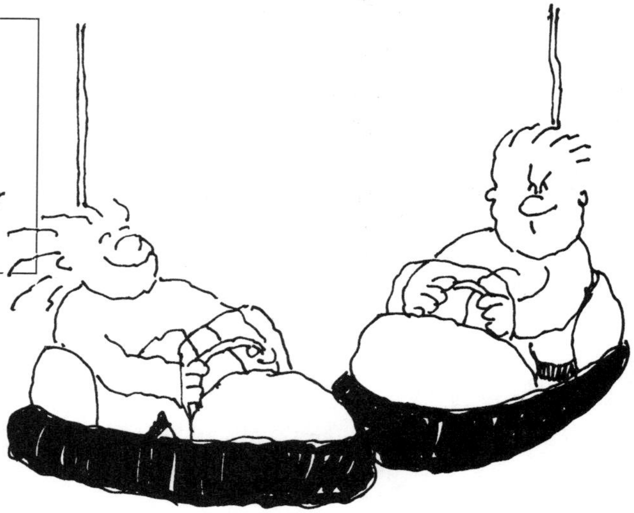

push

poke
prod
jab
nudge

Don't ***poke*** *me in the ribs like that.*

wheel
roll
trundle

Please let me ***wheel*** *the cart around the supermarket.*

press

Press *the black button and the doorbell will ring.*

force
shove
ram

*If you try to **force** any more into that drawer it won't close.*

push

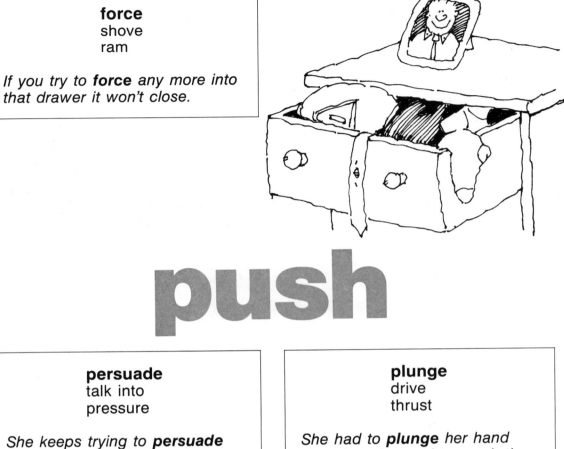

persuade
talk into
pressure

*She keeps trying to **persuade** me to join that awful club of hers.*

plunge
drive
thrust

*She had to **plunge** her hand deep into the mud to reach the ball.*

put

arrange

Arrange *the books on the shelves so the big ones are at the bottom.*

deposit

I'm going to ***deposit*** *some money in the bank.*

dump

Don't ***dump*** *your clothes in a pile on the floor.*

hang

Hang *your coat in the closet.*

lay

Lay *the book on the table.*

load
pile

Load *the bricks into the wheelbarrow.*

place
set

Place *the cup on the saucer.*

position

Position *yourselves at the starting line and wait for the signal.*

rest

Rest *your head on my lap if you're tired.*

stack

Stack *the wood next to the fireplace.*

stand

Stand *the umbrella in the corner.*

put

settle
sit

Settle *yourself in a comfy chair and I'll read you a story.*

stick

Don't ***stick*** *your head out of the car window.*

store
stow

Store *the new books in the cupboard until we need them.*

gentle
placid
easygoing

*This **gentle** horse is the best one for you to ride.*

silent
quiet as a mouse

*Be **silent** or you'll frighten the robin away.*

quiet

Sh!

restful

*Mother and Dad say they need a **restful** weekend at home after working hard all week.*

still
peaceful
calm
hushed
tranquil

*The country is **still** at night, far away from the noisy city.*

shy
timid

*She's very **shy** with people she doesn't know.*

quiet sounds

hiss
hum
murmur
rustle
sigh
swish
tick
tinkle
whisper

correct
proper

*That's not the **correct** key for the lock.*

sensible
responsible

*It was **sensible** of you to run for help.*

right

exact
correct
accurate

*My new watch always has the **exact** time.*

straight
immediately
directly

*We have football training **straight** after school on Mondays.*

honest
fair
decent
proper

*It wouldn't be **honest** to take it without asking.*

suitable
appropriate

*Summer clothes aren't **suitable** for such cold weather.*

climb
ascend

*The stairs **climb** steeply to a small room at the top of the tower.*

increase
go up
jump

*The price of gas will **increase** again next week.*

rise

fly
soar
rocket
take off
shoot
zoom

*We watched the plane **fly** up into the clouds.*

stand up

*We were surprised to see everyone **stand up** and walk out.*

bristly
whiskery
hairy

*Dad's face is **bristly** before he shaves.*

prickly
scratchy

*This bush has very **prickly** leaves.*

rough

bumpy
uneven
rocky

*We had to drive slowly over the **bumpy** road.*

rowdy
wild
boisterous

*If you play **rowdy** games you may get hurt.*

harsh
hoarse
gruff
rasping

*"Get out of here if you know what's good for you," he said in a **harsh** voice.*

stormy
wild
choppy
turbulent

*The boat rocked on the **stormy** sea.*

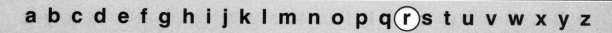

hurry
rush
dash
fly
speed

*We'll have to **hurry** if we want to catch the bus.*

race
sprint

*The crowd cheered as they saw the winner **race** across the finishing line.*

run

jog

*We often **jog** around the park for exercise.*

scurry
scamper
dart

*If you disturb the rabbit it will **scurry** off into its burrow.*

canter

*When horses **canter**, they gallop slowly.*

gallop

*When horses **gallop**, they run at top speed.*

run

flow
stream
pour
wash

*Muddy water **flows** along the gutter after rain.*

stampede
bolt

*The sound of gunfire made the horses **stampede**.*

trot

*When horses **trot**, they go faster than walking but slower than galloping.*

glum
gloomy
mournful

*Something awful must have happened to make her look so **glum**.*

tragic
dreadful
distressing

*Did you hear the **tragic** news about the plane crash?*

sad

heart-broken
grief-stricken

*He was **heart-broken** when his dog was run over.*

unhappy
upset
miserable
depressed
sorry

*She was **unhappy** when her friend left the school.*

careful
cautious
wary

*He's a very **careful** driver and has never had an accident.*

sheltered
protected
secure

*In the cave we were **sheltered** from the storm.*

safe

harmless

*Don't be scared. This type of spider is quite **harmless**.*

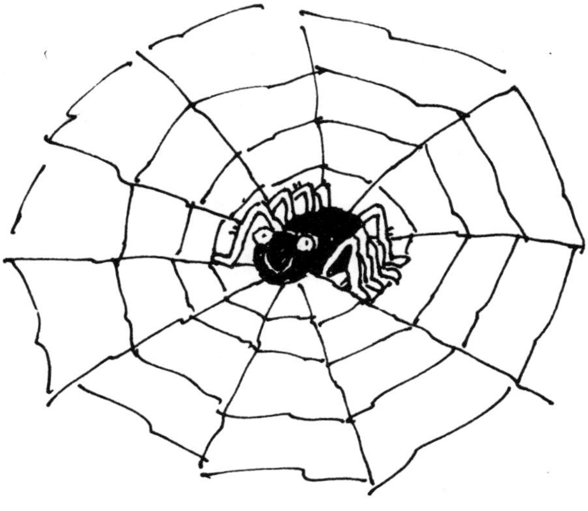

unhurt
unharmed
undamaged
safe and sound

*We found them **unhurt** after they had been lost in the bush for three days.*

announce
declare

*They're going to **announce** the winner's name tomorrow.*

insist

*I am going to **insist** that I am old enough to choose my own clothes.*

say

emphasize
stress
point out

*I must **emphasize** that you need to take extra care crossing this very busy road.*

remark
comment
mention
state

*I heard him **remark** that he had enjoyed the film.*

hint

*I tried to **hint** to my parents that I'd like a BMX bike, but I don't think they understood.*

suggest
propose

*If it's warm this afternoon I **suggest** we should go for a swim.*

pronounce

*You can **pronounce** the word "live" in two different ways.*

recite

*Dad likes to **recite** funny poems to us.*

say

read out
dictate

*I'll **read out** the spelling words and you write them down.*

repeat

*I'll read the first line of the poem, then you **repeat** it.*

reply
answer

*"What's the time?" "Three o'clock," I heard her **reply**.*

There are more words like **say** on the next two pages.

claim

*They **claim** they don't know who broke the window.*

tell
relate
narrate

*I'll look at the pictures while you **tell** the story.*

say

express

*When you're upset it can be hard to **express** how you feel.*

utter

*She was so frightened she couldn't **utter** a sound.*

promise
give your word
swear
vow

*Will you **promise** that you'll never do it again?*

say

different ways you can say things

assert
babble
blurt out
call
chuckle
complain
cry
drawl
exclaim
gasp
grumble
laugh
murmur
mumble
mutter
shout
sigh
snap
snarl
splutter
whine
whimper
whisper
yell

inspect
view

*The estate agent took us to **inspect** three houses that were for sale.*

observe
study
examine

*Astronomers use telescopes to **observe** the stars.*

see

notice

*Did you **notice** that Richard's wearing odd coloured socks?*

spot
recognize
detect

*How many differences can you **spot** in these two drawings?*

watch

*Did you **watch** the baseball on TV last night?*

glance at

I saw her ***glance at*** *it quickly, then turn away.*

peer

We tried to ***peer*** *through the keyhole.*

see

look at

Look at *me! I'm flying!*

peep at
peek at

I tried to ***peep at*** *my sister's diary but she caught me.*

stare at
gaze at

I couldn't help but ***stare at*** *his pink hair.*

dispatch

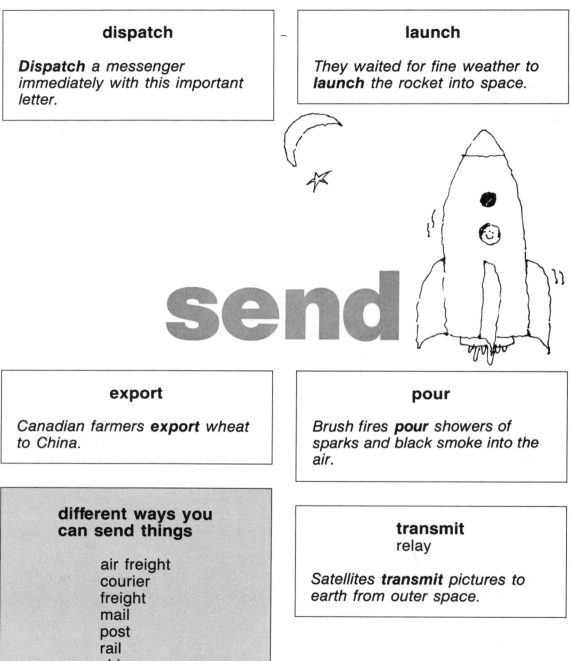

***Dispatch** a messenger immediately with this important letter.*

launch

*They waited for fine weather to **launch** the rocket into space.*

send

export

*Canadian farmers **export** wheat to China.*

pour

*Brush fires **pour** showers of sparks and black smoke into the air.*

different ways you can send things

air freight
courier
freight
mail
post
rail
ship
truck

transmit
relay

*Satellites **transmit** pictures to earth from outer space.*

flutter

*See how the leaves **flutter** in the breeze.*

tremble
shiver
shudder
quiver
quake

*The spooky noises in the dark made us **tremble** with fear.*

shake

rattle
jiggle

***Rattle** the handle if you can't open the door.*

rock
sway

*The explosion made the nearby buildings **rock**.*

vibrate

*The boat began to **vibrate** when the captain started the engine.*

wobble
teeter
totter

*The bike started to **wobble** and I fell off.*

demonstrate

*We asked the man in the shop to **demonstrate** how the video works.*

reveal
uncover
expose

*She rolled up her sleeve to **reveal** a large bruise.*

show

display
exhibit

*We're going to **display** our best paintings for everyone to see.*

teach
tell
explain

*I'll **teach** you how to use the atlas.*

point out
indicate

***Point out** your house to me.*

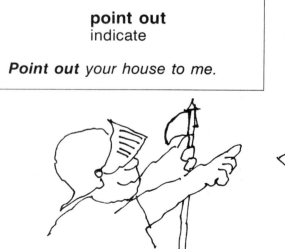

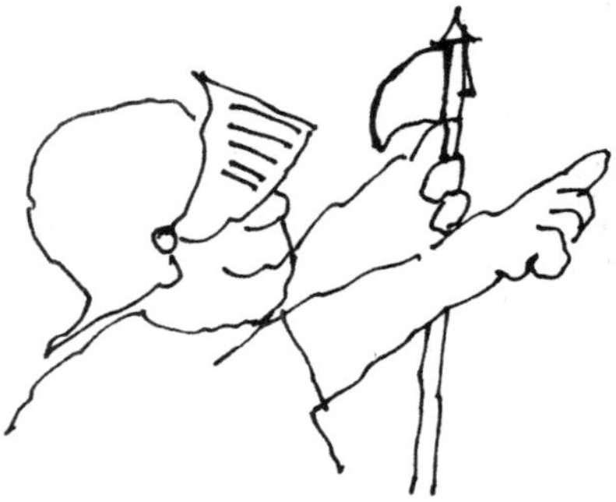

be seen
be visible
be noticeable

*After you wash it, the stain will hardly **be seen**.*

program
picture
film
play

*There's a good **program** on TV tonight.*

show

fair
fete
parade
exhibition
carnival

*Can we go to the **fair** on Saturday?*

prove
confirm

*If you're in the photo it will **prove** that you were there.*

block
bar
seal off

*The construction crew has to **block** the road to repair it.*

closed

*Most shops are **closed** on Sunday.*

shut

close
slam
bang

***Close** the gate so the cows can't get out.*

coast

Take your feet off the pedals and you can ***coast*** *down the hill on your bike.*

skid

Drive slowly! The car might ***skid*** *on this slippery road.*

slip

These socks always ***slip*** *down my legs.*

slide

glide

See how quickly the canoes ***glide*** *through the water.*

slither

I just saw a snake ***slither*** *across the track.*

skate

Watch me ***skate*** *across the ice.*

bumper to bumper

*The cars were moving **bumper to bumper** in the holiday traffic.*

lazily

*The cat woke up and **lazily** stretched its legs.*

slowly

gradually
bit by bit
little by little

*Grandma has been very sick but she is **gradually** getting better.*

sluggishly

*The engine spluttered and the car moved **sluggishly** up the steep hill.*

short
little
wee

*The puppy couldn't climb the stairs on his **short** legs.*

tiny
minute
teeny
teeny-weeny

*You need a magnifying glass to see such a **tiny** insect.*

small

tight
narrow

*The shoes I wore last year are too **tight** now.*

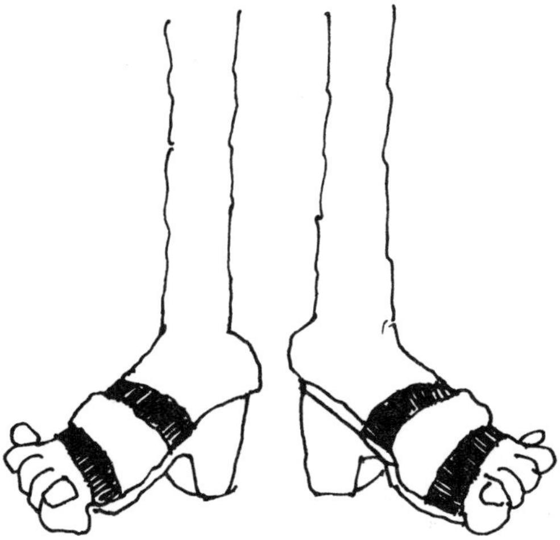

unimportant
slight
minor
trivial

*Don't worry. It was an **unimportant** mistake.*

young
baby

***Young** carrots are sweet and tender.*

calm
comfortable

*The trip across the lake on the ferry was quite **calm**.*

sleek
silky
satiny
velvety

*I like to stroke my kitten's **sleek** fur.*

smooth

creamy

*Spread this **creamy** lotion over your sunburnt skin.*

level
flat
even

*A tennis court needs to be **level** for the balls to bounce properly.*

slippery
polished

*It was hard to get a grip on the **slippery** handle.*

faint
low
slight
feeble

*A **faint** scratching sound came from the cupboard.*

mellow

*A **mellow** glow of candlelight filled the room.*

soft

fluffy
downy

*They wanted to cuddle the **fluffy** little chickens.*

silky

*My hair feels lovely and **silky** after I wash it.*

squashy
mushy
spongy

*The car was bogged in the **squashy** mud.*

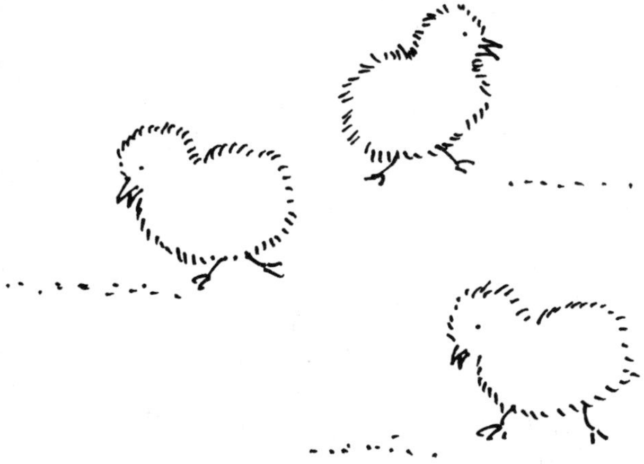

chant words sung in a dull or monotonous singsong voice

folk song a simple song telling of everyday things. Folk songs can be quite old, and at first were not written down.

hit song a song that is played a lot on the radio because many people like it

song

lullaby a song that you sing to put a baby to sleep

national anthem a song praising your country that you sing on important occasions. Canada's national anthem is "O Canada."

nursery rhyme a simple song for very young children

round a song for several singers, each joining in at a different time

begin
commence
open
get going

*When will the show **begin**?*

origin

*The **origin** of the river was high up in the mountains.*

start

beginning

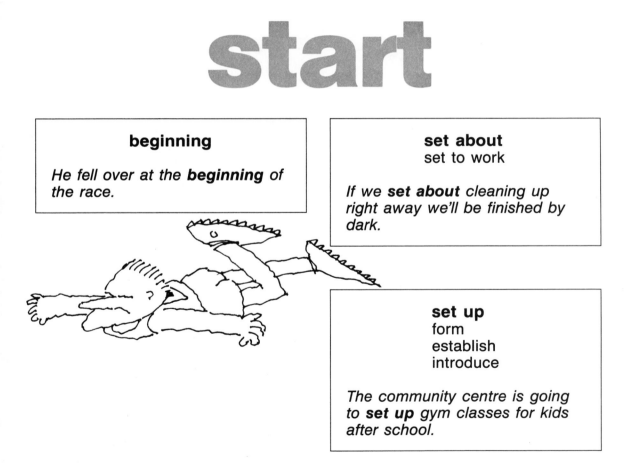

*He fell over at the **beginning** of the race.*

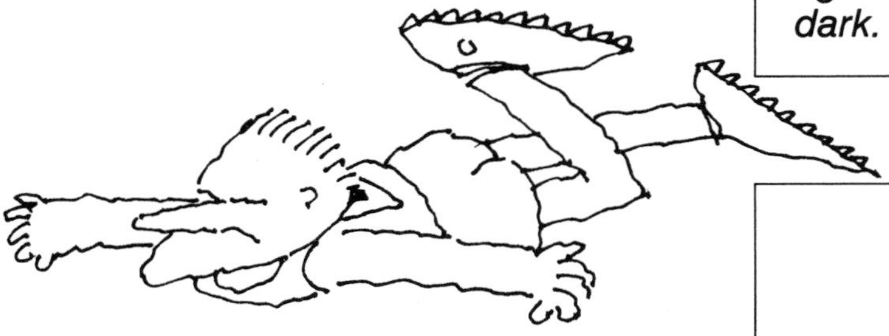

set about
set to work

*If we **set about** cleaning up right away we'll be finished by dark.*

set up
form
establish
introduce

*The community centre is going to **set up** gym classes for kids after school.*

keep
hold

Keep *still while I take your photo.*

stay

linger
loiter

Don't ***linger*** *at the bus stop. Come straight home.*

visit

Our cousins came to ***visit*** *for a week.*

live

We're going to ***live*** *in this house until the end of the year.*

wait
remain
stop

Wait *here while I go to the store.*

finish
end
quit
give up
cease

*We had to **finish** the game when the bell went.*

interrupt
break into

*We **interrupt** this program to bring you a news flash.*

stop

forbid
prohibit
ban

*They are going to put up a sign to **forbid** smoking in the hall.*

pause
break
delay
rest

*There was a short **pause**, then the music started again.*

halt
standstill

*The bus came to a **halt** to let the passengers off.*

prevent
keep

*We put a pillow beside the baby to **prevent** her from rolling off the bed.*

autobiography a story someone writes about his or her own life

biography the story of a person's life

fable a short story with animal characters that teaches about right and wrong

fairytale a story about fairies and magic

story

legend a story from long ago, about famous people and their heroic deeds. Legends are often only partly true.

myth one of the stories about gods, heroes and unusual happenings that were told long ago

parable a religious story that teaches about right and wrong

serial a story in a magazine or on radio or TV that is told one part at a time

tale another name for a story

odd
different
peculiar
queer
unusual
curious

*She has an **odd** way of walking.*

unfamiliar
unknown
unexplored

*They wandered around, lost in an **unfamiliar** part of town.*

strange

weird
crazy
mad

*I had a **weird** dream about swimming in a bowl of soup.*

powerful
mighty
invincible

The country built up a ***powerful*** *army.*

tough
thick
unbreakable

These plates are made of ***tough*** *plastic.*

strong

sturdy
muscular
robust
athletic

He has the ***sturdy*** *body of a weight-lifter.*

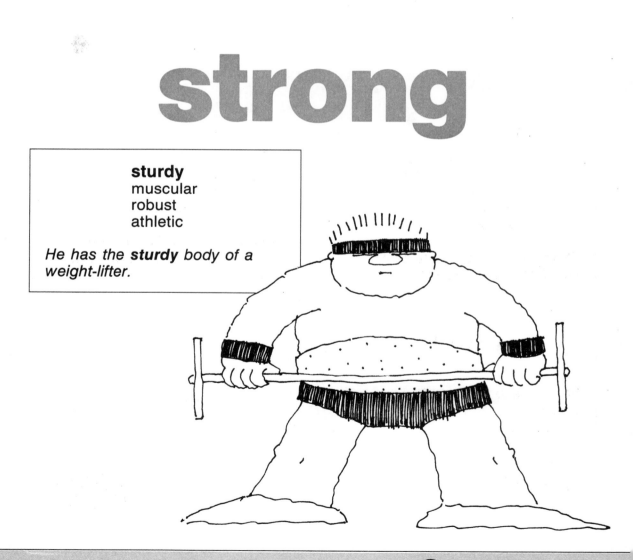

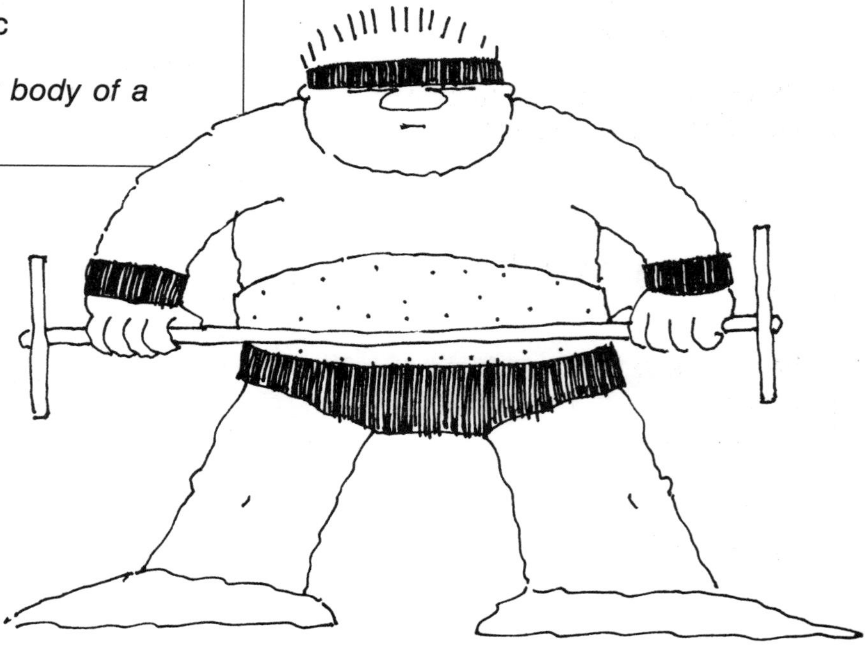

enthusiastic
keen
eager

*They are **enthusiastic** supporters of their local football team.*

strong

overpowering
noticeable
penetrating
pungent

*There was an **overpowering** smell of gas in the room.*

vivid
rich
deep

*I used lots of **vivid** red and purple colours in my painting.*

violent
driving

***Violent** winds blew the trees down.*

dumb
dull
slow
dense
thick

*Our dog is too **dumb** to learn tricks.*

stupid

silly
foolish
senseless
idiotic
reckless

*The **silly** children ran across the road in front of the bus.*

SCHOOL

certain
confident
definite
positive

She was ***certain*** *that she was right.*

sure

firm
secure
steady
solid

The ponies had trouble finding a ***firm*** *footing on the rocky mountain path.*

bring
carry

*You'd better **bring** an umbrella in case it rains.*

hold
grip
grasp
clasp

***Hold** the rope in both hands and pull hard.*

take

confiscate

*The teacher said that if kids brought chewing gum to school he would **confiscate** it.*

remove

*The waiter came to **remove** the dirty plates.*

help yourself to

***Help yourself to** a piece of fruit from the bowl.*

transport
carry
deliver
convey

*There will be buses to **transport** us to the sports ground.*

bear
put up with
tolerate

*He began to cry when he couldn't **bear** the pain any longer.*

steal
pinch
sneak
make off with

*Did you **steal** the money?*

take

need
call for
require

*It will **need** someone with strong hands to get the lid off this bottle.*

snatch
grab
seize

*We saw him **snatch** her bag and run away.*

subtract
deduct

*If you **subtract** 60 from 100 you get 40.*

swallow

*I had to **swallow** some medicine for my cold.*

conversation
chat
discussion

I often have a ***conversation*** *with Grandma on the phone.*

interview

The news reporter had an ***interview*** *with the Prime Minister.*

talk

gossip

They shouldn't ***gossip*** *about my brother because what they say isn't true.*

speak

Hello. Can I ***speak*** *to Simon, please?*

speech
lecture
report

Our principal gave a long ***speech*** *at the assembly.*

coach someone who trains people for football, basketball, swimming and other sports

counsellor a special teacher who helps you if you have problems and are unhappy at school

instructor someone who helps people learn skills such as driving a car, riding a horse, flying a plane and other things like these

teacher

lecturer a teacher at a college or university

principal the teacher in charge of a a school. Other words that can mean the same are **headmaster** and **headmistress**.

professor a teacher at a university

teacher's aid someone whose job is to help a teacher in the classroom

trainer someone who teaches animals to do tricks and to work

tutor a teacher who comes to your house to help you with your school work

advise
warn

*Teachers and parents always **advise** you not to get into cars with strangers.*

narrate

*Lisa couldn't **narrate** the story to the class when she lost her voice.*

tell

inform
advise
notify

*We'll have to **inform** the police that the car's been stolen.*

reveal
confess
admit
divulge
let out

*We forced them to **reveal** their secret hiding place.*

describe
recount
relate

***Describe** how you felt when you were lost in the bush.*

order
command

*"**Order** the slaves to prepare my bath," said the king.*

tell

distinguish

*The twins are so much alike I can't **distinguish** one from the other.*

remind

*I always have to **remind** you to clean your teeth.*

work out
make out
figure out

*Can you **work out** if that's a real gorilla or someone dressed up?*

audition

Fifty people came to the ***audition*** *for the play but only the best ones will be picked.*

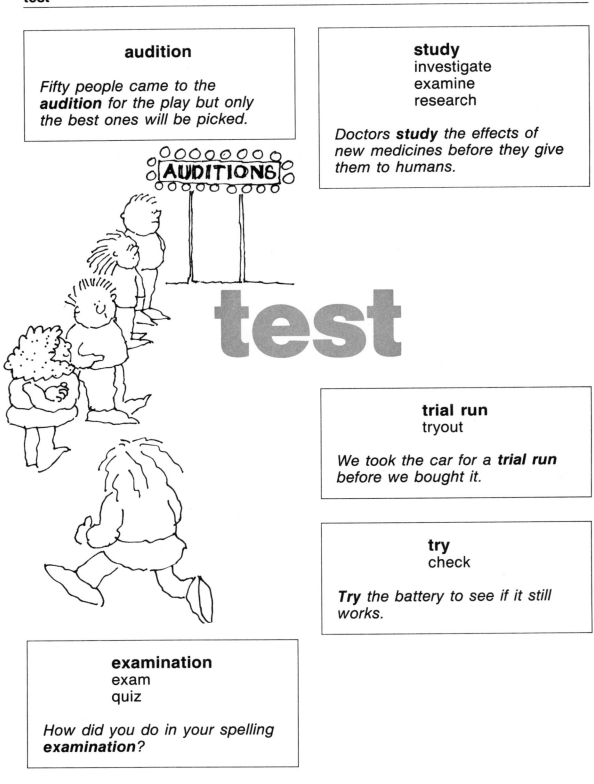

study
investigate
examine
research

Doctors ***study*** *the effects of new medicines before they give them to humans.*

AUDITIONS

test

trial run
tryout

We took the car for a ***trial run*** *before we bought it.*

try
check

Try *the battery to see if it still works.*

examination
exam
quiz

How did you do in your spelling ***examination****?*

fine
flimsy
filmy
paper-thin

*It was such **fine** material it tore very easily.*

skinny
bony
scrawny
gaunt
thin as a rake

*If you don't eat you'll get **skinny**.*

thin

light
scanty
sparse

*There was a **light** cover of snow on the mountain.*

slim
slender
lean

*Playing lots of sport will keep you **slim**.*

narrow

*There was a **narrow** track through the forest.*

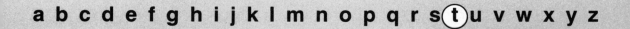

believe
reckon
feel
consider

*I **believe** I could run much faster than you if I tried.*

imagine
wonder
speculate

*I often **imagine** what it would be like to be able to fly.*

think

expect
anticipate

*I didn't **expect** to see you here.*

suppose
suspect
guess

*I **suppose** the robber must have climbed in through the open window.*

concentrate

*I can't **concentrate** with all that noise going on.*

remember
recall
recollect

*I can't **remember** what to do next.*

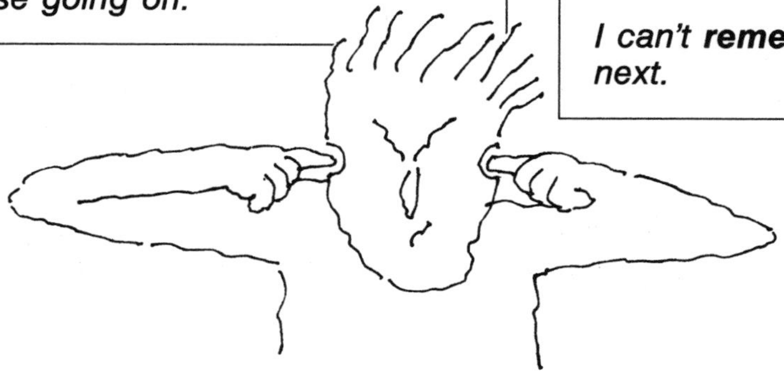

think

judge
conclude

*They'll read all the entries carefully, then say which they **judge** is the best.*

work out
figure out

*I'm trying to **work out** the best thing to do.*

know
realize

*I didn't **know** it was so late. I'd better go home.*

cast

Cast *your fishing line out further away from the pier.*

pass
chuck

Pass *it over here.*

throw

fling
sling
hurl

We watched him ***fling*** *the boomerang high into the air.*

toss
pitch

Let's see who can ***toss*** *the ball the furthest.*

heave

It took two of them to ***heave*** *the great rock into the river.*

different ways you can touch things

brush	poke
graze	rub
hit	scratch
pat	stroke
probe	tap
prod	tickle

handle
finger
fiddle with

*Please don't **handle** the fruit before you buy it.*

touch

feel

*Let me **feel** your forehead to see if you have a fever.*

meet

*Fold the paper so the corners **meet**.*

reach
make contact with

*If I stand on the top bunk I can **reach** the ceiling.*

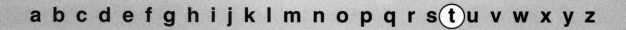

cheat
con
gyp
swindle

*Count the change to make sure they don't **cheat** you out of your money.*

joke
prank

*Do you want to play a **joke** on them by switching their desks?*

trick

fool
deceive
bluff
kid

*I'm going to bandage my arm and **fool** everyone into thinking it's broken.*

knack

*The **knack** to getting the lid off is to squeeze it as you twist it.*

trap
plot
hoax

*They set a clever **trap** to catch the thief.*

honest
truthful
sincere
frank

*Be **honest** and tell me if you like me or not.*

real
genuine
actual
authentic

*It can't be a **real** diamond if it only costs $2.*

true

loyal
faithful
trustworthy
reliable
trusty

*The king chose his most **loyal** soldiers to go with him into battle.*

right
correct
accurate
factual

*Your story about chipmunks building nests in trees isn't **right**.*

YOU
ME?

curve
bend
loop
arch
circle

The new road will ***curve*** *round the old fig tree.*

twist
screw

The bottle top won't come off if you ***twist*** *it the wrong way.*

turn

swing
swerve
veer

When you come to the signpost ***swing*** *sharply to the left.*

wind

Wind *the handle to open the window.*

swivel

Those chairs that ***swivel*** *round are fun to sit on.*

become
go

*Shrimp **become** pink when you cook them.*

go round
spin
whirl
rotate
revolve
twirl

*When you start the engine the wheels **go round**.*

turn

change
convert

*We're going to **change** the verandah into another bedroom.*

try

*Everyone had a **try** on the water slide.*

march

*Can you **march** like soldiers to the beat of the drum?*

stride

*Sometimes in stories giants **stride** across the country, terrifying people.*

walk

parade
strut

*We saw the models **parade** across the room, showing off the new fashions.*

stroll
amble

*They like to **stroll** through the park on a sunny afternoon.*

step

*Watch out or you'll **step** in the mud.*

tiptoe

***Tiptoe** quietly into the room so you don't wake her up.*

dawdle

*Don't **dawdle** or you'll make us late.*

limp
hobble
shuffle

*He could only **limp** because of the blister on his foot.*

walk

hike
tramp

*We plan to **hike** 15 kilometres through the woods.*

stagger
stumble
lurch

*We saw the injured man **stagger** to the side of the road and fall.*

trudge
plod

*We watched him **trudge** wearily up the hill with his heavy bags.*

faint
soft

*We could see the owl in the **faint** light of the moon.*

flimsy
unbelievable
unlikely

*I don't believe her **flimsy** excuse for being late.*

weak

feeble
helpless
frail

*She felt quite **feeble** after two weeks in bed.*

poor

*Bats have very **poor** eyesight.*

damp
moist
sticky
sweaty

*Our T-shirts were **damp** after a hot game of tennis.*

soak
drench
saturate

*If the tent leaks, the rain will **soak** everything.*

wet

dripping
soaked
soaking
wringing wet
drenched

*Our clothes were **dripping** after we were caught in the rain.*

splash
sprinkle
spray
squirt
spatter

*Don't play with the hose near the clothes line or you'll **splash** the dry washing.*

rainy
showery
drizzly

*We play inside on **rainy** days.*

water
hose
irrigate

***Water** the soil well after you plant the seeds.*

be employed

*She used to **be employed** as a cashier at the supermarket.*

job
task
duty
errand
chore

*If you do this **job** for me I'll give you a dollar.*

work

career
job
trade
occupation
profession
business

*What sort of **career** do you want when you grow up?*

slave
struggle
labour
toil

*They had to **slave** for weeks to clean up after the brush fire.*

go
run
play
operate
function

*The radio wouldn't **go** after I dropped it.*

use
drive
run
operate

*Do you know how to **use** the machine?*

false
untrue
inaccurate
misleading

*The robbers gave the police **false** information so they wouldn't be found out.*

mistaken

*I was **mistaken**. Her house is number 3, not number 5.*

unsuitable
inappropriate

*A tiny yard is an **unsuitable** place to keep a big dog.*

wrong

incorrect

*The story was good except for the **incorrect** spelling.*

wicked
criminal
shameful
illegal

*The judge read out a list of all the **wicked** things they had done.*

Appendixes

Baby animals

animal	baby
bear	cub
cat	kitten
bull	calf
cow	calf
deer	fawn
dog	puppy
elephant	calf
hen	chicken
rooster	chicken
goat	kid
goose	gosling
horse	foal
kangaroo	joey
lion	cub
pig	piglet
seal	pup
sheep	lamb
swan	cygnet
whale	calf

Male and female animals

animal	male	female
cattle	bulls	cows
deer	stag	doe
dog	dog	bitch
elephant	bull	cow
fowl	rooster	hen
goat	billy-goat	nanny-goat
goose	gander	goose
duck	drake	duck
lion	lion	lioness
pig	boar	sow
sheep	ram	ewe
tiger	tiger	tigress
whale	bull	cow

Animals' homes

A **dog** sometimes sleeps in a *kennel.*
A **horse** can be kept in a *stable*.
A **pig** can be kept in a *sty*.
A **rabbit** can be kept in an *hutch*.
Birds can be kept in an *aviary*.
Fish can be kept in an *aquarium*.
A **bird** builds a *nest*.
Bees build a *hive*.
A **rabbit** digs a *burrow*.
A **lion** can live in a *den*.
A **bear** can live in a *den*.

Sounds animals make

lions
roar

elephants
trumpet

dogs
bark
bay
growl
howl
snarl
woof
yap
yelp

horses
neigh
whinny

donkeys
bray
heehaw

sheep
baa
bleat

cows and **bulls**
bellow
low
moo

cats
meow
mew
purr

birds
caw
cheep
chirp
coo
hoot
peep
screech
squawk
sing
squeak
trill
tweet
warble

roosters
cock-a-doodle-doo
crow

hens
cackle
cluck

geese
honk

turkeys
gobble

ducks
quack

bees
buzz
drone

pigs
grunt
snort

monkeys
chatter

Groups of animals

a **herd** of cattle or elephants

a **pack** of wolves

a **litter** of kittens or puppies

a **pride** of lions

a **flock** of sheep

a **gaggle** of geese

a **colony** of ants

a **school** or **shoal** of fish

a **swarm** of bees

an **army** of caterpillars

a **pod** of seals

Land features

beach
a sandy or pebbly place at the edge of the sea, where you can play and swim

bush
land in Australia or Africa where the trees and other plants grow wild

canyon
a long narrow valley between mountains with very steep sides. A stream often runs along the bottom. Another word is **gorge**.

cliff
a very steep rocky slope, sometimes at the edge of the sea

coast
the land next to the sea

continent
one of the seven large land masses that we divide the earth into. They are North America, South America, Africa, Europe, Asia, Australia, and Antarctica.

desert
a dry place where very few plants can grow

dune
a long low hill made of sand near the sea or in a desert. It is also called a **sand dune**.

forest
a place where lots of tall trees and other plants grow together

headland
a narrow piece of land that juts out from the coast into the sea

hill
a part of the earth's surface that is higher than the ground around it. It is smaller than a mountain.

island
a piece of land which has water all around it

isthmus
a narrow strip of land with sea on each side connecting two bigger pieces of land. The Isthmus of Panama is an isthmus which joins North America to South America.

jungle
a thick forest in a very warm wet country

mountain
a very large hill with steep high sides that are hard to climb

oasis
a place in a desert with water and trees

peninsula
a long piece of land, almost surrounded by water, that juts out into the sea. The Gaspé Peninsula is a peninsula in Québec.

plateau
a large area of high flat land

prairie
a large area of flat low land without many trees on it. Another word for this is **plain**.

precipice
the very steep side of a cliff or mountain

promontory
a high headland

range
a long line of hills or mountains such as the Laurentians

reef
a long strip of rock, sand or coral just above or below the surface of the sea. The Great Barrier Reef is a reef off the coast of Australia.

shore
the land along the edge of the sea or beside a river or lake

swamp
ground that is soft and wet and usually covered with puddles of muddy water. Another word is **marsh**.

valley
the low flat land between hills or mountains

volcano
a mountain with an opening at the top. Sometimes hot melted rock (called lava), ash, and gases burst out of it from inside the earth.

wood
a small forest

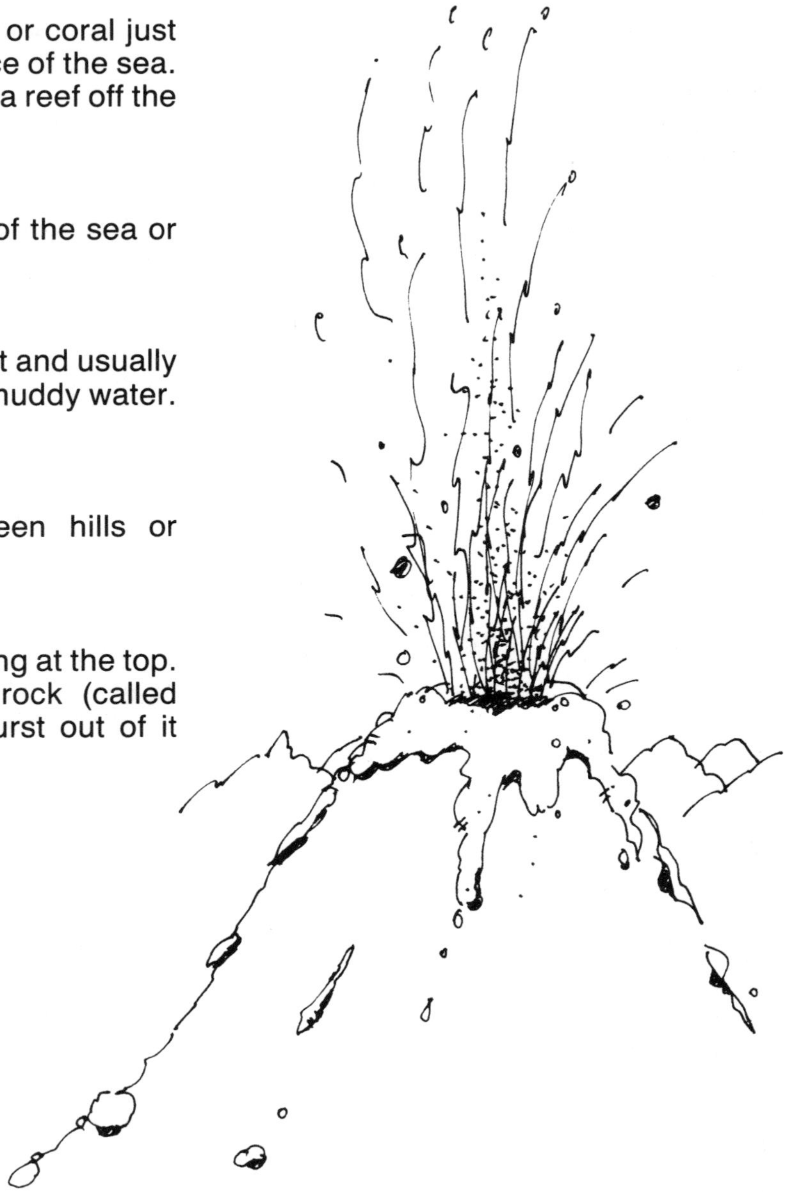

Water features

bay
a curve where water cuts into the shore of a sea or lake

canal
a long narrow waterway built by people for boats

channel
a strip of sea joining two seas. The English Channel is a channel which joins the North Sea to the Atlantic Ocean.

cove
a small bay

creek
a small stream

dam
a strong wall that is built across a river

estuary
the wide part of a river near where it meets the sea

glacier
a large river of ice that moves slowly

gulf
a very large bay. The Gulf of St. Lawrence is a gulf in eastern Canada.

harbour or **harbor**
a bay where the water is deep and calm and ships are safe from the wind and big waves

inlet
a small narrow bay

lagoon
a shallow sea water lake that is separated from the sea by a reef or sandbank

lake
a large area of water with land all around it

ocean
one of the very large areas of salt water that cover the earth, such as the Pacific Ocean or the Atlantic Ocean

pond
a very small lake

pool
a small area of water, especially one you can swim in

river
fresh water that flows in a long winding line across the land

sea
a part of an ocean that is usually near land. The Mediterranean Sea lies between Europe and Africa.

strait
a strip of sea like a channel

stream
a small river

waterfall
a stream or river that flows over the edge of a cliff and falls to the ground below

Quantity . . .

words that tell you how much or how many

few
hardly any
a couple of
a handful of

many
lots of
plenty of
most of
loads of
stacks of
tonnes of

a small amount of
a trace of
a dash of
a scrap of
a pinch of

too much
excess
surplus
waste
unnecessary
extra
additional

not enough
inadequate
insufficient

some
several
various

enough
ample
adequate
sufficient

more than enough
abundant
plentiful

very many
numerous
countless
infinite
umpteen

Time . . .

words that tell you when

always
constantly
continually
continuously
permanently
forever
eternally

again
over and over
repeatedly

now
at once
immediately
right away

later
next
afterwards

earlier
before
already
previously
recently
once
formerly
long ago

often
usually
generally
frequently
regularly

sometimes
seldom
rarely
hardly ever
occasionally
now and then
once in a blue moon

soon
shortly
in a while
presently

never
nevermore

at last
finally
eventually

Index

Aa

abandon leave 87
able good 60–63
about 1
accurate right 119
accurate true 165
ache hurt 78
acquire make 94–95
actual true 165
add up to make 94–95
adjust change 17
admirable good 60–63
adjust change 17
admire like 90
admit tell 156–157
adore like 90
adult big 7
advance move 98–99
adventurous bold 8
advise tell 156–157
advise tell 156–157
afraid frightened 51
aged old 102–103
agreeable good 61
aid help 72
aim mean 96
air freight send 132
airy light 88–89
alarm frighten 50
album book 9
alert bright 12
all right fair 40
allow have 70–71
almost about 1
alter change 17
amazing interesting 80
amazing good 60–63
amble walk 168–169
amend change 17
amount to make 94–95
amusing funny 53
amusing interesting 80
ancient old 102–103
angry 2
announce say 126–129
annoyed angry 2
answer say 127
anticipate think 160–161
antique old 102–103
anxious frightened 51
apartment house 77
appear come 23
appreciate like 90
approach come 23
appropriate right 119
approximately about 1
arch turn 166–167
argue fight 44
argument fight 44
arid dry 35
arrange order 104–105
arrange put 116–117
arrange group 64–65
arrangement order 104–105
arrest catch 16
arrive come 23
arrive get 54–55
as good as gold good 61
ascend climb 21
ascend rise 120
ask 3
ask for order 104–105
assault fight 44
assemble make 94–95
assemble group 64–65
assert say 126–129
assistance help 72
association group 64–65
athletic strong 148–149
atlas book 9
atrocious bad 4–5
attach join 81
attack fight 44
attractive beautiful 6
attractive nice 100–101
audible loud 92–93
audition test 158
authentic true 165

autobiography story 146
average fair 40
award give 56–57
awful bad 4–5
awful hard 68–69
awkward hard 68–69

Bb

babble say 126–129
baby small 139
back go 58–59
backlog pile 110
bad 4–5
bad-tempered angry 2
badly-behaved bad 4–5
bake cook 24
baking hot 76
ban stop 145
bang hit 74–75
bang loud 92–93
bang shut 136
bank pile 110
bar shut 136
barbecue cook 24
bare empty 38
bare clear 19
bash hit 74–75
batch group 64–65
bathe clean 18
battle fight 44
be aware of feel 43
be certain of know 84–85
be confident of know 84–85
be crazy about like 90
be employed work 172
be enough do 32–33
be familiar with know 84–85
be fond of like 90
be mad about like 90
be made up of have 70–71
be noticeable show 134–135
be seen show 134–135
be sufficient do 32–33
be sure of know 84–85
be suspended hang 66
be visible show 134–135
bear take 152–153
bear carry 15
beat hit 74–75
beautiful 6
beautiful nice 100–101
become get 54–55
become go 58–59
become turn 166–167
become a member of join 81
beg ask 3
begin start 143
beginning start 143
believe feel 43
believe think 160–161
belong go 58–59
belt hit 74–75
bend turn 166–167
bicker fight 44
big 7
big old 102–103
biography story 146
bit piece 108–109
bit by bit slowly 138
blank empty 38
blaring loud 92–93
blast loud 92–93
blazing hot 76
blend mix 97
blinding bright 12
blistering hot 76
block shut 136
block out hide 73
blond fair 40
blot out hide 73
bluff trick 164
blunt dull 36
blurt out say 126–129
boil cook 94–95
boiling hot 76
boisterous rough 121
bold 8

bolt run 122–123
bone-dry dry 35
bony thin 159
book 9
boom loud 92–93
boring dull 36
bother disturb 31
bounce jump 82
bound jump 82
boxing match fight 44
brainy clever 20
branch group 64–65
brave bold 8
brawl fight 44
break 10–11
break stop 145
break into stop 145
break up end 39
bright 12
bright clever 20
bright light 88–89
bright clear 19
bright good 60–63
bright happy 67
brilliant bright 12
brilliant clever 20
brimming full 52
bring carry 15
bring move 98–99
bring take 152–153
bring get 54–55
bring about make 94–95
brisk fast 42
bristly rough 121
broken bad 4–5
brush clean 18
brush touch 163
buck jump 82
budge move 98–99
build make 94–95
bulging full 52
bulky big 7
bully frighten 50
bump hit 74–75
bump move 98–99
bump push 114–115
bump into hit 74–75
bumper to bumper slowly 138
bumpy rough 121
bunch group 64–65
bundle group 64–65
buoyant light 88–89
burn light 88–89
burning hot 76
burst break 10–11
bursting at the seams full 52
bury hide 73
business work 172

Cc

cabin house 77
call 13
call say 126–129
call for take 152–153
calm smooth 140
calm quiet 118
camouflage hide 73
can't bear dislike 30
can't stand dislike 30
canter run 122–123
capable good 60–63
capture catch 16
career work 172
carefree bright 12
carefree happy 67
careful safe 125
carefully hard 68–69
careless 14
carnival fair 40
carnival show 134–135
carry 15
carry move 98–99
carry take 152–153
carve cut 26–27
cast throw 162
castle house 77
catch 16

catch fire light 88–89
catch on to follow 49
cause make 94–95
cautious safe 125
cease stop 145
certain sure 151
change 17
change turn 166–167
chant song 142
charming nice 100–101
chase follow 49
chat talk 154
cheat trick 164
check test 158
cheeky bold 8
cheerful happy 67
cheerful bright 12
cheery bright 12
cherish like 90
chew eat 37
chewy hard 68–69
chilly cold 22
chip piece 108–109
choice good 60–63
choice pick 106
choose pick 106
chop cut 26–27
choppy rough 121
chore work 172
chortle laugh 86
christen call 13
chuck throw 162
chuckle laugh 86
chuckle say 126–129
chunk piece 108–109
circle turn 166–167
claim say 128
clamber climb 21
clamour loud 92–93
clasp take 152–153
class group 64–65
clean 18
clean as a whistle clean 18
clear 19
clear loud 92–93
clear plain 111
clear bright 12
clear out empty 38
clear out go 58–59
clever 20
clever good 60–63
climb 21
climb rise 120
clip cut 26–27
clobber hit 74–75
close shut 136
close end 39
closed shut 136
closely hard 68–69
cloudless bright 12
cloudless clear 19
cloudy dull 36
clout hit 74–75
club group 64–65
clump group 64–65
cluster group 64–65
coach teacher 155
coast slide 137
cold 22
collage picture 107
collapse fall 41
collect get 54–55
collect group 64–65
collection pile 110
collection group 64–65
collide with hit 74–75
colossal big 7
colourful or **colorful** bright 12
combine mix 97
come 23
come get 54–55
come across find 45
come after follow 49
come down with catch 16
come together mix 97
come together join 81
come up with find 45
come upon catch 16
come upon find 45
comfortable nice 100–101

comfortable smooth 140
comical funny 53
command order 104–105
command order 104–105
command tell 156–157
commence start 143
comment say 126–129
compel make 94–95
complain say 126–129
complete end 39
complete full 52
complete do 32–33
complicated hard 68–69
comprehend know 84–85
con catch 16
con trick 164
conceal hide 73
concentrate think 160–161
conclude end 39
conclude think 160–161
conclusion end 39
condition order 104–105
condominium house 77
confess tell 156–157
confident sure 151
confirm show 134–135
confiscate take 152–153
connect join 81
consider think 160–161
considerate good 60–63
considerate nice 100–101
consist of have 70–71
construct make 94–95
consult ask 3
contact get 54–55
contain have 70–71
content happy 67
continue go 58–59
continue keep 83
contribute give 56–57
convenient good 60–63
conversation talk 154
convert change 17
convert turn 166–167
convey carry 15
convey give 56–57
convey take 152–153
cook 24
cool cold 22
cool good 60–63
cope with do 32–33
copy 25
copy follow 49
correct right 119
correct right 119
correct true 165
costly good 62
cosy nice 100–101
cottage house 77
counsellor teacher 155
courageous bold 8
courier send 132
courteous good 61
cover up hide 73
crack break 10–11
crack break 10–11
crack up laugh 86
crafty clever 20
crammed full 52
cranky angry 2
crash fall 41
crash loud 92–93
crash into hit 74–75
crawl move 98–99
crazy strange 147
creamy smooth 140
create make 94–95
creep move 98–99
criminal wrong 173
crispy cold 22
add up to make 94–95
cross angry 2
cross-examine ask 3
crowd group 64–65
crowded full 52
cruel mean 96
crumble break 10–11
crummy bad 4–5
crumple fall 41
cry call 13

cry say 126–129
cunning clever 20
cure fix 46
curious funny 53
curious strange 147
curve turn 166–167
cut 26–27
cute beautiful 6

Dd

damage 28
damaging bad 4–5
damp wet 171
dance jump 82
dance move 98–99
dangerous bad 4–5
dangle hang 66
daring bold 8
dart run 122–123
dash run 122–123
dawdle walk 168–169
dawdle move 98–99
dazzling bright 12
deafening loud 92–93
deal with do 32–33
deal with fix 46
deceive trick 164
decent right 119
decide on pick 106
declare say 126–129
decrease fall 41
deduct take 152–153
deep strong 148–149
deface damage 28
defective bad 4–5
defer leave 87
definite sure 151
delay stop 145
delicate light 88–89
delicious nice 100–101
delighted happy 67
delightful nice 100–101
deliver give 56–57
deliver take 152–153
demand order 104–105
demolish damage 28
demonstrate show 134–135
dense stupid 150
depart leave 87
depart go 58–59
depart move 98–99
dependable good 60–63
deposit put 116–117
depressed sad 124
descend fall 41
descent fall 41
describe tell 156–157
desert leave 87
deserted empty 38
despise dislike 30
destroy break 10–11
destroy damage 28
detain keep 83
detect catch 16
detect find 45
detect see 130–131
detest dislike 30
develop catch 16
devoted good 60–63
devour eat 37
diagram picture 107
diary book 9
dictate say 127
dictionary book 9
different strange 147
difficult hard 68–69
din loud 92–93
dine eat 37
dip fall 41
direct order 104–105
directly right 119
dirty 29
disagreement fight 44
disappear go 58–59
disastrous bad 4–5
discover catch 16
discover find 45

discover find 45
discussion talk 154
disgraceful bad 4–5
disguise hide 73
dislike 30
dismal dull 36
disobedient bad 4–5
disobey break 10–11
dispatch send 132
display show 134–135
distant lonely 91
distinguish tell 156–157
distinguished important 79
distress disturb 31
distressing sad 124
disturb 31
disturb move 98–99
division group 64–65
divulge tell 156–157
do 32–33
donate give 56–57
downy soft 141
drab dull 36
drag pull 112–113
drain empty 38
drain flow 47
drape hang 66
draw pull 112–113
draw near come 23
drawing picture 107
drawl say 126–129
dreadful bad 4–5
dreadful sad 124
dreary dull 36
drench wet 171
drenched wet 171
dribble flow 47
drift fly 48
drift pile 110
drink 34
drip flow 47
dripping wet 171
drive push 114–115
drive work 172
driving strong 148–149
drizzly wet 171
droop hang 66
drop fall 41
drop move 98–99
dry 35
dull 36
dull stupid 150
dumb stupid 150
dump put 116–117
duplicate copy 25
dust clean 18
dusty dirty 29
duty work 172

Ee

eager strong 148–149
early old 102–103
earn get 54–55
earn make 94–95
ear-splitting loud 92–93
easygoing quiet 118
eat 37
elderly old 102–103
elegant beautiful 6
elegant nice 100–101
emphasize say 126–129
empty 38
empty clear 19
encyclopedia book 9
end 39
end stop 145
ending end 39
enjoy like 90
enjoyable nice 100–101
enjoyable good 61
enormous big 7
enquire ask 3
enrol in join 81
enter join 81
entertaining interesting 80

entertaining good 61
enthusiastic strong 148–149
entire full 52
erect make 94–95
errand work 172
escape go 58–59
essential important 79
establish start 143
even smooth 140
everyday plain 111
evident clear 19
evil bad 4–5
exact right 119
exam test 158
examination test 158
examine see 130–131
examine test 158
excellent good 61
exceptional good 61
exchange change 17
exciting interesting 80
exciting good 61
exclaim say 126–129
exercise book book 9
exhausting hard 68–69
exhibit show 134–135
exhibition fair 40
exhibition show 134–135
exit leave 87
expect think 160–161
expensive good 62
experience feel 43
experience have 70–71
experience know 84–85
experienced good 60–63
expert clever 20
expert good 60–63
explain show 134–135
explode break 10–11
export send 132
expose show 134–135
express fast 42
express say 128
exquisite beautiful 6
exquisite nice 100–101
extend go 58–59
extensive big 7

Ff

fable story 146
fabulous good 60–63
factual true 165
faint soft 141
faint weak 170
fair 40
fair show 134–135
fair right 119
fairytale story 146
faithful true 165
fake copy 25
fall 41
fall move 98–99
false wrong 173
famous important 79
fancy like 90
fare do 32–33
fascinating good 61
fascinating interesting 80
fashionable nice 100–101
fast 42
fasten join 81
faulty bad 4–5
fearful frightened 51
fearless bold 8
fed up angry 2
feeble weak 170
feeble soft 141
feed on eat 37
feel 43
feel touch 163
feel know 84–85
feel think 160–161
festival fair 40
fetch get 54–55
fetch call 13

fete fair 40
fete show 134–135
feverish hot 76
fiddle with touch 163
fiery hot 76
fight 44
figure out find 45
figure out tell 156–157
figure out think 160–161
film show 134–135
filmy thin 159
filthy dirty 29
finale end 39
finalize end 39
find 45
find catch 16
find out ask 3
fine clear 19
fine light 88–89
fine nice 100–101
fine thin 159
fine good 60–63
finger touch 163
finish do 32–33
finish end 39
finish stop 145
firm hard 68–69
firm sure 151
firmly fast 42
first-class good 61
first-rate good 60–63
fit go 58–59
fix 46
fix get 54–55
fix make 94–95
flake piece 108–109
flaming hot 76
flap fly 48
flare light 88–89
flash light 88–89
flat dull 36
flat smooth 140
flee go 58–59
flicker light 88–89
flimsy weak 170
flimsy light 88–89
flimsy thin 159
fling throw 162
flit fly 48
float fly 48
floating light 88–89
flog hit 74–75
flood flow 47
flow 47
flow run 122–123
fluffy soft 141
flutter fly 48
flutter shake 133
fly 48
fly rise 120
fly move 98–99
fly run 122–123
folk song song 142
follow 49
follow keep 83
fool catch 16
fool trick 164
foolish stupid 150
forbid stop 145
force make 94–95
force push 114–115
forceful hard 68–69
forgery copy 25
forgetful careless 14
form make 94–95
form start 143
former old 102–103
foul bad 4–5
foul dirty 29
fracture break 10–11
fragment piece 108–109
frail weak 170
frank true 165
free-for-all flight 44
freezing cold 22
freight send 132
fresh cold 22
friendly nice 100–101

frighten 50
frightened 51
frightful bad 4–5
frosty cold 22
frozen cold 22
fry cook 24
full 52
fully-grown big 7
function work 172
funny 53
furious angry 2

Gg

gain get 54–55
gallop run 122–123
gang group 64–65
gap break 10–11
gash cut 26–27
gasp say 126–129
gather group 64–65
gather pick 106
gather get 54–55
gaudy bright 12
gaunt thin 159
gaze at see 130–131
generous nice 100–101
gentle quiet 118
genuine true 165
get 54–55
get go 58–59
get make 94–95
get along do 32–33
get going start 143
get ready make 94–95
giant big 7
gifted clever 20
gigantic big 7
giggle laugh 86
give 56–57
give leave 87
give a hand help 72
give away give 56–57
give birth to have 70–71
give up stop 145
give your word say 126–129
glad happy 67
glamorous beautiful 6
glamorous nice 100–101
glance at see 130–131
glare light 88–89
glaring bright 12
gleam light 88–89
gleaming bright 12
glide slide 137
glide fly 48
glimmer light 88–89
glint light 88–89
glisten light 88–89
glistening bright 12
glitter light 88–89
glittering bright 12
gloomy dull 36
gloomy sad 124
glorious nice 100–101
glorious beautiful 6
glow light 88–89
glum sad 124
go 58–59
go work 172
go around turn 166–167
go away move 98–99
go by air fly 48
go by plane fly 48
go forward move 98–99
go on keep 83
go out leave 87
go through have 70–71
go up rise 120
gobble eat 37
good 60–63
good important 79
good nice 100–101
good-looking beautiful 6
good-natured nice 100–101
gorgeous beautiful 6

gossip talk 154
grab catch 16
grab take 152–153
grade group 64–65
gradually slowly 138
grasp catch 16
grasp take 152–153
graze eat 37
graze touch 163
greasy dirty 29
great big 7
great good 60–63
greedy mean 96
grey dull 36
grief-stricken sad 124
grill cook 24
grimy dirty 29
grip take 152–153
gripping good 61
group 64–65
grow get 54–55
grow go 58–59
grown-up big 7
grown-up old 102–103
grubby dirty 29
gruff rough 121
grumble say 126–129
grumpy angry 2
guard keep 83
guess think 160–161
gulp drink 34
gush flow 47
guzzle drink 34
gyp trick 164

Hh

hack cut 26–27
hairy rough 121
halt stop 145
hammer hit 74–75
hand over give 56–57
handle touch 163
handle do 32–33
handsome beautiful 6
handsome nice 100–101
handy good 60–63
hang 66
hang put 116–117
happen come 23
happy 67
happy bright 12
hard 68–69
harm hurt 78
harmful bad 4–5
harmless safe 125
harsh loud 92–93
harsh rough 121
harvest pick 106
hassle disturb 31
hate dislike 30
haul pull 112–113
have 70–71
have a row fight 44
have a soft spot for like 90
have in mind mean 96
have learned know 84–85
have met know 84–85
hazardous bad 4–5
heal fix 46
healthy good 62
heap pile 110
hear catch 16
heart-broken sad 124
heave throw 162
heave pull 112–113
heavy big 7
help 72
help yourself to take 152–153
helpful good 60–63
helpful nice 100–101
helping piece 108–109
helpless weak 170
heroic bold 8
hide 73
high-speed fast 42

hike walk 168–169
hilarious funny 53
hint say 126–129
hiss quiet 118
hit 74–75
hit move 98–99
hit touch 163
hit song song 142
hitch pull 112–113
hoard pile 110
hoarse rough 121
hoax trick 164
hobble walk 168–169
hold keep 83
hold take 152–153
hold stay 144
hole break 10–11
holler call 13
homesick lonely 91
honest right 119
honest true 165
hop jump 82
hop move 98–99
horrible bad 4–5
hose wet 171
hot 76
hot good 60–63
hot and bothered angry 2
house 77
hover fly 48
howl loud 92–93
huge big 7
huge big 7
hum quiet 118
humorous funny 53
hungry empty 38
hunk piece 108–109
hunt follow 49
hurdle jump 82
hurl throw 162
hurried fast 42
hurry run 122–123
hurry move 98–99
hurt 78
hurt angry 2
hush up hide 73
hushed quiet 118
hut house 77

Ii

icy cold 22
identify know 84–85
idiotic stupid 150
ignite light 88–89
illegal wrong 173
illuminate light 88–89
illustration picture 107
imagine think 160–161
imitate follow 49
imitate copy 25
imitation copy 25
immaculate good 62
immediately right 119
immense big 7
impersonate copy 25
impertinent bold 8
important 79
improve help 72
impudent bold 8
inaccurate wrong 173
inappropriate wrong 173
incorrect wrong 173
increase rise 120
indicate mean 96
indicate show 134–135
inform tell 156–157
injure hurt 78
insist say 126–129
insist order 104–105
insolent bold 8
inspect see 130–131
instruct order 104–105
instruction order 104–105
instructor teacher 155
insulted hurt 78

intelligent clever 20
intend mean 96
intense bad 4–5
intently hard 68–69
interesting 80
interesting good 61
interfere with disturb 31
intermission break 10–11
interrogate ask 3
interrupt stop 145
interrupt disturb 31
interview talk 154
intimidate frighten 50
intriguing interesting 80
introduce start 143
invent make 94–95
investigate test 158
invincible strong 148–149
irrigate wet 171
irritable angry 2
isolated lonely 91
issue give 56–57

Jj

jab push 114–115
jammed full 52
jerk pull 112–113
jiggle shake 133
jittery frightened 51
job work 172
job work 172
jog run 122–123
join 81
joke trick 164
jolly happy 67
jostle push 114–115
journey go 58–59
joyful happy 67
judge think 160–161
jumble mix 97
jump 82
jump move 98–99
jump rise 120
just fair 40
just about about 1

Kk

keen strong 148–149
keep 83
keep have 70–71
keep stay 144
keep stop 145
keep secret hide 73
kid trick 164
kill yourself laughing laugh 86
kind good 60–63
kind nice 100–101
kind make 94–95
knack trick 164
knock hit 74–75
knock move 98–99
knock push 114–115
know 84–85
know think 160–161
know feel 43

Ll

labour work 172
lap drink 34
large big 7
last old 102–103
laugh 86
laugh say 126–129
launch send 132
lay put 116–117
lazily slowly 138
leak flow 47
lean thin 159
leap jump 82

learn do 32–33
learn find 45
leave 87
leave go 58–59
leave move 98–99
lecture talk 154
lecturer teacher 155
legend story 146
lend a hand help 72
lessen fall 41
let out tell 156–157
level smooth 140
level group 64–65
lift move 98–99
light 88–89
light thin 159
light fair 40
light as a feather light 88–89
light-hearted happy 67
like 90
like a flash fast 42
like lightning fast 42
limp walk 168–169
linger stay 144
link join 81
little small 139
little by little slowly 138
live stay 144
lively bright 12
lively fast 42
load put 116–117
load pile 110
loathe dislike 30
locate find 45
loiter stay 144
lonely 91
lonesome lonely 91
look after keep 83
look at see 130–131
look down on dislike 30
loop turn 166–167
loud 92–93
love like 90
lovely beautiful 6
lovely nice 100–101
low soft 141
loyal good 60–63
loyal true 165
lug pull 112–113
lukewarm hot 76
lullaby song 142
lump piece 108–109
lurch walk 168–169
luscious nice 100–101

Mm

mad angry 2
mad strange 147
mail send 132
make 94–95
make get 54–55
make a present of give 56–57
make better help 72
make contact with touch 163
make head or tail of follow 49
make off with take 152–153
make out tell 156–157
make out catch 16
make your blood run cold frighten 50
make your flesh creep frighten 50
make your hair stand on end frighten 50
manage do 32–33
mansion house 77
manual book 9
manufacture make 94–95
march walk 168–169
mardi gras fair 40
marvellous good 61
mash mix 97
mass pile 110
match fight 44
mature old 102–103
mature big 7
mean 96

meddle with disturb 31
meet join 81
meet touch 163
mellow soft 141
mend fix 46
mention say 126–129
merge mix 97
merry bright 12
merry happy 67
mess up damage 28
messy dirty 29
messy careless 14
mighty big 7
mighty strong 148–149
mild hot 76
mild nice 100–101
mimic copy 25
mind keep 83
mingle mix 97
minor small 139
minute small 139
mischievous bad 4–5
miserable bad 4–5
miserable dull 36
miserable sad 124
miserly mean 96
misleading wrong 173
mistaken wrong 173
mix 97
mob group 64–65
model copy 25
modify change 17
moist wet 171
monotonous dull 36
mop clean 18
more or less about 1
mound pile 110
mount climb 21
mountain pile 110
mournful sad 124
move 98–99
move disturb 31
move carry 15
mow cut 26–27
muddy dirty 29
mumble say 126–129
munch eat 37
mural picture 107
murmur quiet 118
murmur say 126–129
muscular strong 148–149
mushy soft 141
must have 70–71
mutter say 126–129
myth story 146

Nn

nail hang 66
name call 13
narrate tell 156–157
narrate say 128
narrow thin 159
narrow small 139
nasty bad 4–5
nasty mean 96
national anthem song 142
naughty bad 4–5
nearly about 1
necessary important 79
need have 70–71
need take 152–153
nervous frightened 51
nibble eat 37
nice 100–101
nice good 60–63
nick cut 26–27
nickname call 13
nippy cold 22
noisy loud 92–93
not bad fair 40
notice see 130–131
notice feel 43
notice find 45
noticeable strong 148–149
notify tell 156–157
novel book 9

nudge push 114–115
nursery rhyme song 142

Oo

obey keep 83
object to dislike 30
objectionable bad 4–5
observe see 130–131
observe find 45
observe keep 83
obtain get 54–55
obtain make 94–95
obvious clear 19
obvious plain 111
occupation work 172
occupied full 52
occur come 23
odd strange 147
odd funny 53
offended angry 2
offensive bad 4–5
offer give 56–57
old 102–103
old-fashioned old 102–103
olden old 102–103
ooze flow 47
open start 143
opening break 10–11
operate work 172
oppose fight 44
order 104–105
order ask 3
order tell 156–157
ordinary plain 111
organize group 64–65
organize order 104–105
origin start 143
ought have 70–71
out-of-the-way lonely 91
outcome end 39
outstanding good 61
overcast dull 36
overflow flow 47
overflowing full 52
overjoyed happy 67
overpowering strong 148–149
own have 70–71

Pp

pack group 64–65
packed full 52
painting picture 107
palace house 77
pale light 88–89
pale fair 40
panic-stricken frightened 51
paper-thin thin 159
parable story 146
parade walk 168–169
parade show 134–135
parched dry 35
part piece 108–109
part group 64–65
pass throw 162
pass on give 56–57
passable fair 40
past old 102–103
pastel light 88–89
pat touch 163
patch fix 46
pattern picture 107
pattern order 104–105
pause stop 145
peaceful quiet 118
peculiar funny 53
peculiar strange 147
peek at see 130–131
peep at see 130–131
peer see 130–131
penetrating strong 148–149
peppery hot 76
perfect good 62
perform do 32–33
persuade push 114–115

pester disturb 31
petrified frightened 51
phone call 13
photo picture 107
photocopy copy 25
pick 106
pick up get 54–55
picture 107
picture show 134–135
piece 108–109
piercing loud 92–93
pile 110
pile put 116–117
pilot fly 48
pin hang 66
pinch take 152–153
pitch throw 162
place put 116–117
place have 70–71
placid quiet 118
plain 111
plain clear 19
plan mean 96
play do 32–33
play show 134–135
play work 172
plead ask 3
pleasant good 61
pleasant nice 100–101
pleased happy 67
plod walk 168–169
plot trick 164
pluck pick 106
plunge push 114–115
plunge fall 41
point out show 134–135
point out say 126–129
poke push 114–115
poke touch 163
polish clean 18
polished smooth 140
polite good 61
polluted dirty 29
poor bad 4–5
poor weak 170
pop break 10–11
portion piece 108–109
portrait picture 107
position put 116–117
positive sure 151
possess have 70–71
post send 132
poster picture 107
pounce jump 82
pound hit 74–75
pour flow 47
pour send 132
pour run 122–123
powerful strong 148–149
powerful hard 68–69
powerful loud 92–93
practically about 1
prance jump 82
prank trick 164
precious good 62
prefer like 90
prehistoric old 102–103
prepare get 54–55
prepare make 94–95
present give 56–57
press push 114–115
pressure push 114–115
pretty beautiful 6
pretty nice 100–101
prevent stop 145
previous old 102–103
prickly rough 121
principal teacher 155
probe touch 163
proceed move 98–99
prod push 114–115
prod touch 163
produce have 70–71
produce make 94–95
profession work 172
professor teacher 155
program show 134–135
prohibit stop 145

prominent important 79
promise say 126–129
pronounce say 127
proper right 119
propose mean 96
propose say 126–129
protected safe 125
prove show 134–135
provide give 56–57
prune cut 26–27
pull 112–113
pull move 98–99
punch hit 74–75
pungent strong 148–149
pursue follow 49
push 114–115
push move 98–99
put 116–117
put keep 83
put have 70–71
put off leave 87
put out angry 2
put together make 94–95
put up make 94–95
put up with have 70–71
put up with take 152–153

Qq

quake shake 133
quarrel fight 44
quarrel fight 44
queer funny 53
queer strange 147
question ask 3
quick fast 42
quick clever 20
quickly fast 42
quiet 118
quiet as a mouse quiet 118
quit leave 87
quit stop 145
quiver shake 133
quiz ask 3
quiz test 158

Rr

race run 122–123
racket loud 92–93
raid fight 44
rail send 132
rainy wet 171
ram push 114–115
rapid fast 42
rapidly fast 42
rasping rough 121
rattle shake 133
raucous loud 92–93
raw cold 22
reach touch 163
reach get 54–55
reach go 58–59
read out say 127
real true 165
realize find 45
realize know 84–85
realize think 160–161
reap pick 106
rear jump 82
reasonable fair 40
recall know 84–85
recall think 160–161
receive get 54–55
recite say 127
reckless stupid 150
reckon think 160–161
recognize know 84–85
recognize see 130–131
recollect know 84–85

recollect think 160–161
recount tell 156–157
regarding about 1
relate say 128
relate tell 156–157
relay send 132
reliable good 60–63
reliable true 165
remain stay 144
remark say 126–129
remarkable interesting 80
remember know 84–85
remember think 160–161
remind tell 156–157
remodel change 17
remote lonely 91
remove move 98–99
remove pick 106
remove take 152–153
reorganize change 17
repair fix 46
repair order 104–105
repeat say 127
replace change 17
replica copy 25
reply say 127
report talk 154
request ask 3
require take 152–153
research test 158
resent dislike 30
resign leave 87
resist fight 44
respect like 90
responsible right 119
rest break 10–11
rest put 116–117
rest stop 145
restful quiet 118
result end 39
retire leave 87
retreat go 58–59
return go 58–59
reveal show 134–135
reveal tell 156–157
revise change 17
revolve turn 166–167
rich strong 148–149
ridiculous funny 53
right 119
right fair 40
right true 165
rigid hard 68–69
rinse clean 18
rip break 10–11
rise 120
rise move 98–99
risky bad 4–5
roam go 58–59
roar loud 92–93
roar with laughter laugh 86
roast cook 24
robust strong 148–149
rock shake 133
rocket rise 120
rocky rough 121
roll move 98–99
roll push 114–115
rotate turn 166–167
rotten bad 4–5
rough 121
roughly about 1
round song 142
row fight 44
row loud 92–93
rowdy rough 121
rub touch 163
ruckus loud 92–93
rude bold 8
ruin break 10–11
ruin damage 28
rumble loud 92–93
rumpus loud 92–93
run 122–123
run move 98–99
run work 172

run away go 58–59
rush run 122–123
rustle quiet 118

Ss

sad 124
safe 125
safe and sound safe 125
sail move 98–99
satiny smooth 140
satisfactory fair 40
satisfied happy 67
saturate wet 171
save keep 83
saw cut 26–27
say 126–129
scale climb 21
scamper run 122–123
scanty thin 159
scare frighten 50
scared frightened 51
scared stiff frightened 51
scared to death frightened 51
scatterbrained careless 14
scorching hot 76
scorn dislike 30
scour clean 18
scramble climb 21
scramble mix 97
scrap piece 108–109
scrape cut 27
scratch touch 163
scratchy rough 121
scrawny thin 159
screw turn 166–167
scrub clean 18
scrumptious nice 100–101
scuffle fight 44
scurry run 122–123
seal off shut 136
second-rate bad 4–5
section group 64–65
section piece 108–109
secure join 81
secure safe 125
secure sure 151
securely fast 42
see 130–131
see find 45
see know 84–85
see-through clear 19
seem feel 43
seep flow 47
seize catch 16
seize take 152–153
select pick 106
selection pick 106
selfish mean 96
send 132
send for call 13
sensational good 60–63
sense feel 43
senseless stupid 150
sensible right 119
sequence order 104–105
serial story 146
serious bad 4–5
serve help 72
set group 64–65
set put 116–117
set hard 68–69
set about start 143
set off go 58–59
set to work start 143
set up start 143
settle put 116–117
settle end 39
severe bad 4–5
shabby old 102–103
shadow follow 49
shake 133
shameful wrong 173
shape order 104–105
share piece 108–109
sharp clever 20
sharp cold 22
shatter break 10–11

shear cut 26–27
sheltered safe 125
shift carry 15
shift disturb 31
shift move 98–99
shimmer light 88–89
shining bright 12
shiny bright 12
ship send 132
shiver shake 133
shock frighten 50
shocking bad 4–5
shoddy bad 4–5
shoot up rise 120
short small 139
should have 70–71
shout call 13
shout say 126–129
shove push 114–115
show 134–135
show fair 40
show mean 96
show up come 23
showery wet 171
shred piece 108–109
shrewd clever 20
shriek loud 92–93
shrill loud 92–93
shrivel dry 35
shudder shake 133
shuffle mix 97
shuffle walk 168–169
shut 136
shy quiet 118
sick to death angry 2
side group 64–65
sigh quiet 118
sigh say 126–129
sign up with join 81
silent quiet 118
silky soft 141
silky smooth 140
silly stupid 150
simple clear 19
simple plain 111
sincere true 165
sinister bad 4–5
sink fall 41
sip drink 34
sit put 116–117
skate slide 137
sketch picture 107
skid slide 137
skilful clever 20
skilful good 60–63
skilled good 60–63
skilled clever 20
skinny thin 159
skip jump 82
skip move 98–99
slab piece 108–109
slam shut 136
slap hit 74–75
slapdash careless 14
slash cut 26–27
slave work 172
sleek smooth 140
slender thin 159
slice cut 26–27
slice piece 108–109
slide 137
slide move 98–99
slight small 139
slight soft 141
slim thin 159
sling throw 162
slip slide 137
slip fall 41
slippery smooth 140
slit cut 26–27
slit break 10–11
slither slide 137
slither move 98–99
sliver piece 108–109
sloppy careless 14
slow stupid 150
slowly 138
slug hit 74–75
sluggishly slowly 138
slurp drink 34

smack hit 74–75
small 139
smart clever 20
smart good 60–63
smart hurt 78
smash break 10–11
smash damage 28
smash into hit 74–75
smirk laugh 86
smooth 140
snap break 10–11
snap say 126–129
snappy angry 2
snarl say 126–129
snatch take 152–153
snatch catch 16
sneak take 152–153
sneak away go 58–59
sneer laugh 86
snicker laugh 86
snip cut 26–27
soak wet 171
soaked wet 171
soaking wet 171
soar fly 48
soar rise 120
society group 64–65
sock hit 74–75
soft 141
soft weak 170
solid hard 68–69
solid sure 151
solitary lonely 91
solve fix 46
song 142
sorry sad 124
sort group 64–65
sort make 94–95
sort order 104–105
sort out order 104–105
spank hit 74–75
sparkle light 88–89
sparkling clean 18
sparse thin 159
spatter wet 171
speak talk 154
special important 79
speculate think 160–161
speech talk 154
speed run 122–123
speedily fast 42
speedy fast 42
spell break 10–11
spicy hot 76
spill flow 47
spin turn 166–167
spiteful mean 96
splash wet 171
splendid beautiful 6
splendid good 60–63
splinter piece 108–109
splinter break 10–11
split cut 26–27
split break 10–11
split your sides laugh 86
splutter say 126–129
spoil damage 28
spoiled bad 4–5
sponge clean 18
spongy soft 141
spot see 130–131
spot find 45
spotless clean 18
spray wet 171
spread go 58–59
spring jump 82
sprinkle wet 171
sprint run 122–123
spurt flow 47
squabble fight 44
squashy soft 141
squirt flow 47
squirt wet 171
stack pile 110
stack put 116–117
stagger walk 168–169
stampede run 122–123
stand put 116–117
stand have 70–71
stand up rise 120

standstill stop 145
stare at see 130–131
start 143
startle frighten 50
stash hide 73
state order 104–105
state say 126–129
stay 144
steady sure 151
steal take 152–153
step walk 168–169
stew cook 24
stick put 116–117
sticky wet 171
stiff hard 68–69
still quiet 118
sting hurt 78
stingy mean 96
stir mix 97
stir move 98–99
stop 145
stop end 39
stop stay 144
store put 116–117
store keep 83
stormy rough 121
story 146
stow put 116–117
stow keep 83
straight right 119
straightforward clear 19
strain pull 112–113
strange 147
strange funny 53
stream flow 47
stream fly 48
stream run 122–123
stress say 126–129
stretch go 58–59
stride walk 168–169
strike hit 74–75
stroke touch 163
stroll walk 168–169
strong 148–149
strong hard 68–69
strong loud 92–93
struggle work 172
strut walk 168–169
study test 158
study do 32–33
study see 130–131
stumble fall 41
stumble walk 168–169
stupid 150
sturdy strong 148–149
style make 94–95
stylish nice 100–101
subtract take 152–153
suck drink 34
suggest say 126–129
suitable good 60–63
suitable right 119
sulky angry 2
summery hot 76
summon call 13
sunbaked dry 35
sunny bright 12
sunny clear 19
super good 60–63
superb good 60–63
supply give 56–57
support carry 15
support help 72
suppose think 160–161
suppose think 160–161
sure 151
surge flow 47
surprise catch 16
suspect think 160–161
swallow take 152–153
swap change 17
sway shake 133
swear say 126–129
sweaty wet 171
sweep clean 18
sweet beautiful 6
sweet nice 100–101
swerve turn 166–167
swift fast 42
swiftly fast 42

swindle trick 164
swing turn 166–167
swing hang 66
swish quiet 118
switch change 17
swivel turn 166–167
swoop fly 48

Tt

tack hang 66
tail follow 49
take 152–153
take carry 15
take pick 106
take away move 98–99
take off rise 120
take place come 23
taken full 52
tale story 146
talented clever 20
talk 154
talk into push 114–115
tap hit 74–75
tap touch 163
task work 172
taste eat 37
tasty nice 100–101
tattered old 102–103
teach show 134–135
teacher 155
teacher's aid teacher 155
team group 64–65
tear break 10–11
tear pull 112–113
tedious dull 36
teeny small 139
teeny-weeny small 139
teeter shake 133
telephone call 13
tell 156–157
tell order 104–105
tell say 128
tell show 134–135
terrible bad 4–5
terrific good 60–63
terrified frightened 51
terrify frighten 50
terrorize frighten 50
test 158
textbook book 9
the very best good 62
thesaurus book 9
thick strong 148–149
thick stupid 150
thin 159
thin as a rake thin 159
think 160–161
thirsty dry 35
thoughtful good 60–63
thoughtful nice 100–101
thrash hit 74–75
thrilled happy 67
thrilling good 61
thrilling interesting 80
throb hurt 78
throng group 64–65
throw 162
throw move 98–99
thrust push 114–115
thump hit 74–75
thunder loud 92–93
thunderous loud 92–93
tick quiet 118
tickle touch 163
tie join 81
tight small 139
tightly fast 42
timid frightened 51
timid quiet 118
tinkle quiet 118
tiny small 139
tip end 39
tiptoe walk 168–169
tiring hard 68–69
titter laugh 86
toast cook 24
toil work 172

tolerate have 70–71
tolerate take 152–153
top good 61
topple over fall 41
toss throw 162
total make 94–95
totter shake 133
touch 163
touch feel 43
touch hit 74–75
tough hard 68–69
tough strong 148–149
tow pull 112–113
townhouse house 77
trace copy 25
trace find 45
track follow 49
track down find 45
trade work 172
traditional old 102–103
tragic sad 124
trail hang 66
trainer teacher 155
tramp walk 168–169
tranquil quiet 118
transfer move 98–99
transfer change 17
transform change 17
transmit send 132
transparent clear 19
transport take 152–153
transport carry 15
trap trick 164
trap catch 16
travel go 58–59
travel move 98–99
travel at do 32–33
treasure like 90
tremble shake 133
trial run test 158
trick 164
trick catch 16
trickle flow 47
tricky hard 68–69
trim cut 26–27
trip fall 41
trivial small 139
trot run 122–123
trouble disturb 31
truck send 132
trudge walk 168–169
true 165
true good 60–63
trundle push 114–115
trustworthy true 165
trusty true 165
truthful true 165
try turn 166–167
try test 158
tryout test 158
tug pull 112–113
tumble fall 41
tumult loud 92–93
turbulent rough 121
turn 166–167
turn change 17
turn out make 94–95
turn over give 56–57
turn up come 23
tutor teacher 155
twinkle light 88–89
twirl turn 166–167
twist turn 166–167
type make 94–95

Uu

unattractive plain 111
unbelievable weak 170
unbreakable strong 148–149
uncomplicated clear 19
uncover show 134–135
undamaged good 62
undamaged safe 125
understand follow 49
understand get 54–55
understand know 84–85
uneven rough 121

unexplored strange 147
unfamiliar strange 147
unhappy sad 124
unhappy bad 4–5
unhappy lonely 91
unharmed safe 125
unhurt safe 125
unimportant small 139
uninhabited empty 38
uninteresting dull 36
unkind mean 96
unknown strange 147
unlikely weak 170
unoccupied empty 38
unpleasant hard 68–69
unpleasant bad 4–5
unsafe bad 4–5
unspoiled good 62
unsuitable wrong 173
untidy careless 14
untrue wrong 173
unusual funny 53
unusual strange 147
uproar loud 92–93
upset disturb 31
upset hurt 78
upset angry 2
upset sad 124
use work 172
used old 102–103
useful good 60–63
utter say 128

Vv

vacant empty 38
vacuum clean 18
valuable good 62
valuable important 79
value like 90
vandalize damage 28
vanish go 58–59
vary change 17
vast big 7
veer turn 166–167
velvety smooth 140
vibrate shake 133
view see 130–131
vile bad 4–5
vintage old 102–103
violent strong 148–149
visit come 23
visit stay 144
vivid strong 148–149
vivid bright 12
vow say 126–129

Ww

wait stay 144
walk 168–169
walk move 98–99
wallop hit 74–75
wander go 58–59
want like 90
war fight 44
warm hot 76
warm nice 100–101
warn tell 156–157
wary safe 125
wash clean 18
wash run 122–123
watch see 130–131
water wet 171
weak 170
wedge piece 108–109
wee small 139
weighty big 7
weird strange 147
weird funny 53
welcome good 61
well-behaved good 61
well-mannered good 61
wet 171
whack hit 74–75
wheel push 114–115

whimper say 126–129
whine say 126–129
whip hit 74–75
whirl turn 166–167
whiskery rough 121
whisper say 126–129
whisper quiet 118
whole full 52
wholesome good 62
wicked bad 4–5
wicked wrong 173
wide-awake bright 12
wild angry 2
wild rough 121
win get 54–55
wind turn 166–167
wintry cold 22
wish for like 90
wither dry 35
witty funny 53
wobble shake 133
wolf down eat 37
wonder think 160–161
wonderful good 61
wonderful nice 100–101
work 172
worked up angry 2
work out find 45
work out tell 156–157
work out think 160–161
work out follow 49
worn-out old 102–103
worried frightened 51
worry disturb 31
wound hurt 78
wreck break 10–11
wreck damage 28
wrench pull 112–113
wrestling match fight 44
wriggle move 98–99
wringing wet wet 171
wrong 173

Yy

yank pull 112–113
year group 64–65
yell call 13
yell say 126–129
young small 139
yummy nice 100–101

Zz

zoom rise 120

Guide to the index

The index helps you find any word in the thesaurus, whether it is a **keyword**, a **heading word** or a **similar word**. Like all indexes, this one is set out in alphabetical order, with page numbers.

Look at the index on the opposite page and find *hurt*. Did you notice that it appears twice?

The first time *hurt* is written it is in blue printing. This means it is a **keyword**. It can be found on page 78 of the thesaurus, along with many other words which have a similar meaning.

The second time *hurt* is written it is in ordinary black printing, followed by angry in blue printing. This means that you can find *hurt* among the words that are similar to angry on page 2. Look at page 2. *Hurt* is with **sulky**, **put out** and **offended**.

The words in the index that are in heavy black printing are **heading words**. Look at *hurry* on the opposite page. It is the heading of a group of words that are similar to run on pages 122–123.

Can you work out why *hold* is in the index three times? It is because it is the heading of a group of words that mean keep on page 83; it is also the heading of a group of words that mean take on pages 152–153; and it is also in a group of words that mean stay on page 144.

Look them up in the thesaurus and make up sentences using *hold* in these three different ways.

hit 74–75
hit **move** 98–99
hit **touch** 163
hit song **song** 142
hitch **pull** 112–113
hoard **pile** 110
hoarse **rough** 121
hoax **trick** 164
hobble **walk** 168–169
hold **keep** 83
hold **take** 152–153
hold **stay** 144
hole **break** 10–11
page number
holler **call** 13
homesick **lonely** 91
honest **right** 119
honest **true** 165
hop **jump** 82
hop **move** 98–99
similar word
horrible **bad** 4–5
hose **wet** 171
hot 76
hot and bothered **angry** 2
house 77
hover **fly** 48
howl **loud** 92–93
huge **big** 7
huge **big** 7
hum **quiet** 118
humorous **funny** 53
hungry **empty** 38
hunk **piece** 108–109
hunt **follow** 49
hurdle **jump** 82
hurl **throw** 162
hurried **fast** 42
heading word
hurry **run** 122–123
hurry **move** 98–99
keyword
hurt 78
hurt **angry** 2
keyword
hush up **hide** 73
hushed **quiet** 118
hut **house** 77